IN TRANSLATION
The Strange Character Options

CREDITS

Writer/Designer	Bruce R. Cordell
Developer	Monte Cook
Creative Director	Shanna Germain
Editor and Proofreader	Ray Vallese
Cover Artist	Matt Stawicki
Graphic Designer	Bear Weiter

Artists Jacob Atienza, Marco Caradonna, Nicholas Cloister, Sam Cullum, Dreamstime.com, David Hueso, Baldi Konijn, Guido Kuip, Brandon Leach, Eric Lofgren, Grzegorz Pedrycz, Mike Perry, John Petersen, Michael Phillippi, Roberto Pitturru, Joe Slucher, Lee Smith, Matt Stawicki, Cyril Terpent, Cory Trego-Erdner, Tiffany Turrill, Shane Tyree, Cathy Wilkins

Monte Cook Games Editorial Board Scott C. Bourgeois, David Wilson Brown, Eric Coates, Gareth Hodges, Jeremy Land, Laura Wilkinson, Marina Wold, George Ziets

TABLE OF CONTENTS

INTRODUCTION

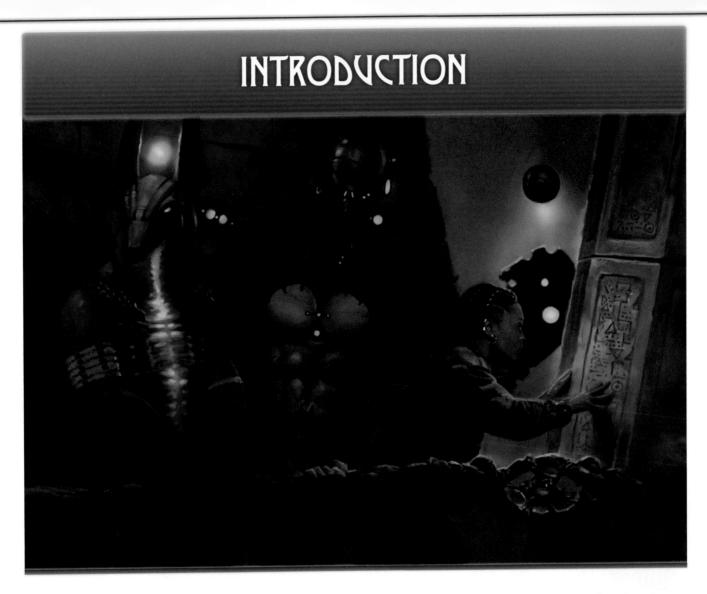

Foci, page 26

In Translation is crammed with more options for creating new characters, options for advancing existing characters to higher tiers, and perhaps most important, additional foci for existing characters when they translate between recursions. In fact, *In Translation* more than doubles the number of foci presented in *The Strange* corebook. That's important for several reasons.

When a player character begins playing The Strange, she starts from a single recursion, which is probably Earth. Because only some of all the foci in the corebook are available in any given recursion, the PC chooses her focus from a limited subset. So even though about thirty foci are presented in *The Strange* corebook, a PC starting on Earth can choose from only about eight of them. With *In Translation*, which introduces more than thirty new foci, that's now opened up.

That said, PCs in The Strange have the opportunity to gain additional foci each time they translate, which is another reason why *In Translation* was needed. Characters will go through foci at a much higher rate over the course of a campaign than in another Cypher System game where a PC's focus remains static over the same period. More foci means that player characters have more potential to remain differentiated as they adventure amid the limited worlds of Magic, Mad Science, Standard Physics, and more.

Pilots Starcraft, page 69

Throws Boulders, page 88

In addition, foci are a great way for players (and GMs) to learn more about the recursion where the foci are offered, even if indirectly. For example, it says something about a recursion if a character can choose Pilots Starcraft as opposed to Throws Boulders.

Finally, it was important to create more foci because, essentially, foci are cool.

One of the biggest challenges in writing *In Translation* was coming up with more interesting foci for Earth, especially when foci like Soars Across the Sky and Aspires to Be Posthuman are available. Lots of Earth professions are too narrow, too limited, or—let's face it—too boring to interest a player. The discerning question we had to ask ourselves was, "Would a tier 6 ability of a proposed Earth focus stack up reasonably well against a tier 6 ability from an Ardeyn or Ruk focus?" If the answer was no, that focus concept was discarded. Thankfully, after some brainstorming and deep thinking, we're thrilled with what we've come up with for new Earth foci, and we think you will be too.

Besides foci, *In Translation* offers new descriptors, including Introverted, Crazy, Spiritual, and Slacker.

Last but not least, the Character Type Options chapter offers tons of new special abilities for paradoxes, spinners, and vectors.

So there you have it: a big book of new options designed to give your characters years of additional fun exploring the recursions of The Strange!

Soars Across the Sky, page 83

Aspires to Be Posthuman, page 29

Descriptors, page 15

Introverted, page 18

Crazy, page 17

Spiritual, page 24

Slacker, page 24

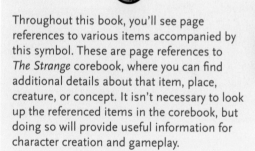

Throughout this book, you'll see page references to various items accompanied by this symbol. These are page references to *The Strange* corebook, where you can find additional details about that item, place, creature, or concept. It isn't necessary to look up the referenced items in the corebook, but doing so will provide useful information for character creation and gameplay.

I AM AN *ADJECTIVE NOUN* WHO *VERBS*

As a reminder, creating your character for The Strange comes down to building a simple sentence: "I am a [fill in an adjective here] [fill in a noun here] who [fill in a verb here]." Thus: "I am an *adjective noun* who *verbs*."

For example, you might say, "I am a Meticulous spinner who Aspires to Be Posthuman" or "I am a Crazy paradox who Manipulates Strange Energy."

In this sentence, the adjective is your *descriptor*.

The noun is your character *type*.

The verb is your *focus*.

For complete details on creating a character for The Strange, including stats, tiers, skills, character sheets, and a character creation walkthrough, see *The Strange* corebook (especially Part 2: Character Creation).

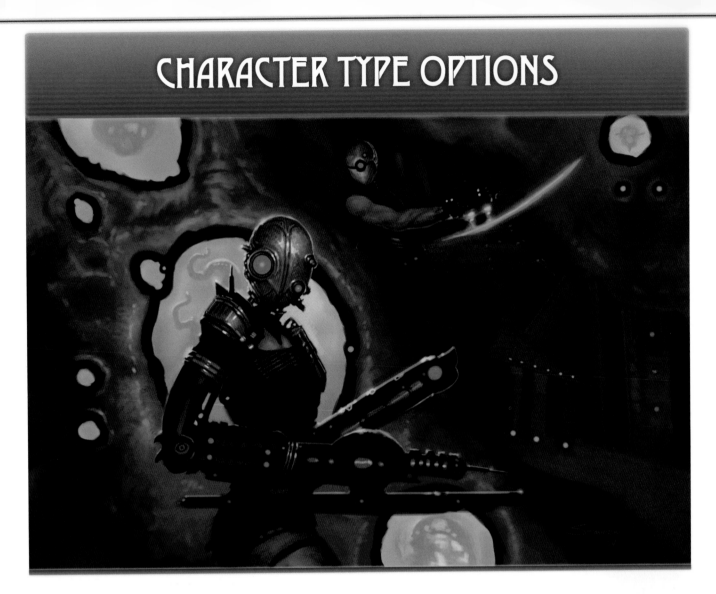

Pool, page 16

Edge, page 17

Effort, page 17

If you play a vector, paradox, or spinner in The Strange, the total number of moves, revisions, and twists you can choose from each tier just expanded.

Using Special Abilities: Using these abilities often costs points from your stat Pools. The cost is listed in parentheses after the ability name. Your Edge in the appropriate stat can reduce the cost of the ability, but remember that you can apply Edge only once per action.

Sometimes the point cost for an ability has a + sign after the number. For example, the cost might be given as "2+ Intellect points." That means you can spend more points or more levels of Effort to improve the ability further.

Many special abilities grant a character the option to perform an action that she couldn't normally do, such as summoning an object from a recursion or attacking multiple foes at once. Using one of these abilities is an action

unto itself, and the end of the ability description says "Action" to remind you. It also might provide more information about when or how you perform the action.

Some special abilities allow you to perform a familiar action—one that you can already do—in a different way. For example, an ability might let you weather mental effects, gain mastery over routine tasks, or inflict damage if attacking someone from the shadows. These abilities are called enablers. Using one of these abilities is not considered an action. Enablers either function constantly (such as being able to wear heavy armor, which isn't an action) or happen as part of another action (such as summoning an object to your hand immediately before using the object as your normal action). If a special ability is an enabler, the end of the ability's description says "Enabler" to remind you.

VECTOR: NEW MOVES

Vectors can add these new special abilities to the list when selecting their moves for each tier.

FIRST·TIER VECTOR

Control the Field (1 Might point): This melee attack inflicts 1 less point of damage than normal, but regardless of whether you hit the target, you maneuver it into a position you desire within immediate range. Action.

Move Like the Wind (3 Speed points): When you call on your reserves, you can move a long distance each round as your turn. If you also have the Fleet of Foot move and you use Move Like the Wind, if you succeed at a difficulty 2 Speed roll to run, you can move a long distance and take an action in the same round (in that order). Action.

Opportunist: You have an asset on any attack roll you make against a creature within immediate range that has been attacked at some point during the round by someone else. Enabler.

SECOND·TIER VECTOR

Drop Out (2 Might points): You enter into a deathlike trance so deep that you appear to be dead for up to one day. During this time you do not need food or water, and you have +5 to Armor against the effects of cold, fire, vacuum, or other extreme effects of the environment. Against damage from attacks, this same benefit grants you +2 to Armor, though a direct attack also shocks you out of your trance. You are not aware of your surroundings while you've dropped out. Action to initiate.

Mighty Blow (2 Might points): You strike two foes with a single blow. Make separate attack rolls for each foe, but both attacks count as a single action in a single round. You remain limited by the amount of Effort you can apply on one action. Anything that modifies your attack or damage applies to both of these attacks. Action.

Fleet of Foot, page 26

Ignore the Pain,
page 28

Recovery roll, page 108

Sidestep Detonation: You have an uncanny ability to avoid ground zero for explosive attacks, such as those created by grenade detonations or similar effects. Even if you fail a Speed defense roll to avoid such an attack, you gain +2 to Armor against the damage that particular attack inflicts. Enabler.

THIRD · TIER VECTOR

From the Shadows: If you successfully attack a creature that was previously unaware of your presence, you deal 3 additional points of damage. Enabler.

Reaction: If a creature you attacked on your last turn with a melee attack uses its action to move out of immediate range, you gain an action to attack the creature as a parting blow, even if you have already taken a turn in the round. Enabler.

Seize the Moment (4+ Speed points): If you succeed on a Speed defense roll to resist an attack, you gain an action. You can use the action immediately even if you have already taken a turn in the round. You don't take an action during the next round, unless you apply a level of Effort when you use Seize the Moment. Enabler.

FOURTH · TIER VECTOR

Momentum: If you use an action to move, your next attack made using a melee weapon before the end of the next round inflicts 2 additional points of damage. Enabler.

Opening Gambit (4 Might points): Your melee attack shreds the defenses of a target. Any energy-based defenses it has (such as a force field or mental ward) are negated for 1d6 + 1 rounds. If the creature has no energy-based defenses, its Armor is reduced by 2 for one minute. If it has no energy-based defenses or Armor, the difficulty of all attacks made against the creature is lowered by one step for one minute. Action.

Tough As Nails: When you are impaired or debilitated, the difficulty of Might-based tasks and defense rolls you attempt is decreased

Characters can't apply Effort or other moves, such as Bash, to any task they accomplish using Tough As Nails.

Bash, page 26

by one step. If you also have Ignore the Pain, make a difficulty 1 Might defense roll when you reach 0 points in all three of your Pools to immediately regain 1 Might point and avoid dying. Each time you attempt to save yourself with this ability before your next ten-hour recovery roll, the difficulty increases by one step. Enabler.

FIFTH · TIER VECTOR

Assassinate (5 Intellect points): If you successfully attack a creature that was previously unaware of your presence, you deal 9 additional points of damage. Enabler.

Improved Success: When you roll a 17 or higher on an attack roll that deals damage, you deal an additional point of damage. For instance, if you roll a natural 18, which normally deals 2 extra points of damage, you deal 3 extra points instead. If you roll a natural 20 and choose to deal damage instead of achieve a special major effect, you deal 5 extra points of damage. Enabler.

Take Command (3 Intellect points): You draw upon your presence and authority as a vector to issue a specific command to an ally. On the ally's turn, if it chooses to listen to your command, the difficulty of any task or attack it attempts is reduced by one step, and it deals 3 additional points of damage. Action.

SIXTH · TIER VECTOR

Magnificent Moment: If you make an attack or attempt a task with the immediate action you gain by using Seize the Moment, the difficulty is reduced by one step. Enabler.

Wild Vitality (4 Intellect points): You attune with the life force of a natural creature (your size or bigger) within long range that you can see. This is a level 2 Intellect task. If you succeed, the creature is not harmed, but through resonance with its wild vitality, you gain several benefits for up to one minute: an asset to all your Might-based tasks (including attacks and defenses), +2 to your Might Edge and Speed Edge, and 2 additional points of damage on all successful melee attacks. Action to initiate.

PARADOX: NEW REVISIONS

Paradoxes can add these new special abilities to the list when selecting their revisions for each tier.

FIRST·TIER PARADOX

Anomalous Pulse (1 Intellect point): A target within long range is subject to a disorienting, brain-jarring pulse of energy that deals 1 point of damage that ignores Armor. On a successful attack, in addition to the damage, the difficulty of all actions attempted by the target on its next turn increases by one step. Action.

Disperse Strange Energy (2 Intellect points): An ongoing effect created by a cypher within short range ends. If the effect is affecting a creature, you must succeed on an Intellect-based attack to end it. Action.

Entangling Force (1+ Intellect point): A target within short range is subject to a snare constructed of semi-tangible lines of force for one minute. The force snare is a level 2 construct. A target caught in the force snare cannot move from its position, but it can attack and defend normally. The target can also spend its action attempting to break free. You can apply Effort to increase the level of the force snare by 1 per level of Effort applied. Action to initiate.

SECOND·TIER PARADOX

Concussive Blast (2 Intellect points): You release a beam of pure force that smashes into a creature within short range, inflicting 5 points of damage and moving it an immediate distance farther back. Action.

Mental Link (1+ Intellect point): You open a pathway to another creature's mind via a light touch, which allows you to transmit thoughts and images to each other. You can communicate without having to speak, though communication is vastly improved if you both speak the same language. The mental link remains regardless of distance (but not across recursion boundaries) and lasts for one hour. Instead of applying Effort to decrease the difficulty, you can extend the duration by one hour for each level of Effort applied.

If you apply a level of Effort when you use this ability on an intelligent target that doesn't share your language, you can communicate with the target reasonably well. Action to initiate.

Summon From Recursion (3 Intellect points): An object that you've previously designated and prepared instantly appears in your hand. The object must be small enough to fit in your hand. This is a difficulty 2 Intellect-based task. Preparing a designated object requires that you use this power on it as you place it in a secure location you've set aside, such as a locked chest, safe, or treasury. If the object is moved after you've prepared and secured it, you lose your link to it. You can have up to three prepared items at the same time. Enabler.

Disperse Strange Energy could reintroduce to the timestream the target of a stasis keeper, strip away the asset to Speed defense rolls granted by a temporary shield, make visible the subject of a vanisher, or eliminate the ability of a water adapter user to breathe underwater, for example.

THIRD-TIER PARADOX

Down the Rabbit Hole (5 Intellect points): You create a temporary inapposite gate to a nascent recursion that is a pocket dimension. The recursion is no larger than 225 square feet (21 square meters) and has characteristics determined by the GM, but it's essentially a safe place for you and any allies who accompany you to rest for up to twelve hours. The gate to the pocket recursion is invisible to anyone but you and those you designate. The gate dissolves twelve hours after you create it with this revision. As is true of any recursion, once you've visited, you can return via normal translation if you wish. Using Down the Rabbit Hole connects to a completely

Inapposite gate, page 135

Pocket dimension, page 142

If a linked creature tries to reject a particular instance of contact from an imbued communication fetish, the contact initiator can force the link to be established by succeeding on an Intellect attack, but the difficulty of the attack is increased by one step.

different recursion each time, the same one as previously, or a mix, at the GM's discretion. Action.

Fling (4 Intellect points): You violently launch a creature or object about your size or smaller within short range and send it flying a short distance in any direction. This is an Intellect attack that inflicts 4 points of damage to the object being flung when it lands or strikes a barrier. If you aim the primary target at another creature or object (and succeed on a second attack), the secondary target also takes 4 points of damage. Action.

Imbue Communication Fetish (6 Intellect points): You imbue an object with the permanent ability to serve as a mental link between a single creature and whomever is touching the object, regardless of distance (even across recursion boundaries). Both the creature and the object must be within immediate range of you when you imbue the object. The subject creature must be intelligent enough to be able to communicate using language. The object can be no larger than you (such as a sculpture, a large painting, or a mirror) and no smaller than a key fob, a figurine, or a playing card. The link allows the object holder and the linked creature to transmit thoughts and images (and, potentially, mental attacks) to each other. Action to imbue, action to initiate link.

FOURTH-TIER PARADOX

Matter Cloud (5 Intellect points): Pebbles, dirt, sand, and debris rise into the air around you to form a swirling cloud. The cloud extends out to immediate range and moves with you. The cloud remains around you for ten minutes. When it ends, all the materials fall to the ground around you. The cloud makes it harder for other creatures to attack you. You have an asset on all Speed defense rolls until the effect ends.

In addition, while the cloud is around you, you can use an action to whip the material so that it abrades everything within immediate range. Each creature and object in the area takes 2 points of damage. Action to initiate.

Sift the Worlds (5+ Intellect points): When you initiate a translation, instead of translating into a known recursion, you can attempt to draw an unliving, untended, and mundane object to wherever you are. You describe the general parameters of the object you are looking for, and the GM determines what appears if you are successful. The object you produce from fiction appears through an inapposite gate, is (usually) level 5, and could be a weapon, a small vehicle, a piece of art, a chest of gold, and so on (though nothing larger than could fit in a 10-foot [3 m] cube). This is a difficulty 5 translation roll. Instead of applying Effort to decrease the difficulty, you can apply four levels of Effort to attempt to draw an artifact from a world that operates under a different law than the recursion where you attempt Sift the Worlds. For example, if you're on Earth and you attempt to produce a magic sword from Ardeyn (as opposed to a regular sword), you must apply four levels of Effort. Objects that operate under a different law begin to degrade in usefulness after a minute. Four hours to initiate the translation; two hours to initiate if hastened by another character; ten minutes to initiate if hastened by another character who's a spinner.

Translation Ward (4+ Intellect points): You ward an area no larger than a long distance across, making it more difficult to translate into that location. You do so by raising the effective level of the area by 1 plus the level of the recursion hosting the area. This is a difficulty 2 Intellect-based task. Instead of applying Effort to decrease the difficulty, you can apply Effort to increase the level of the ward. Thus, to increase the effective level of the warded area by 4 (three levels above the normal limit), you must apply three levels of Effort. Action.

As a separate use, you can also use Translation Ward to permanently redirect those who fail to translate into an area you warded. When you do this within 1 mile (1.6 km) of the warded area, recursors who attempt and fail to translate into the warded area are not subject to an effect from the Translation Failure table, but instead appear in an area that you choose within immediate range. Action.

FIFTH-TIER PARADOX

Armor of Atrocity (6+ Intellect points): Regardless of the recursion you currently inhabit, you and your equipment become rimed with hellish frost from the recursion of Hell Frozen Over for one minute. The rime grants you +5 to Armor against all attacks. When a creature successfully strikes you, you choose whether to instantly discharge a portion of the rime to automatically inflict 5 points of damage to your foe (which also decreases Armor by 1 with each use). Each level of Effort applied increases Armor by 1 and the revenge damage by 1 point. Action.

Divide Your Mind (7 Intellect points): You split your consciousness into two parts. For one minute, you can take two actions on each of your turns, but only one of them can be to make an attack of any kind. Action.

Dust to Dust (7 Intellect points): You disintegrate one nonliving object smaller than you and whose level is less than or equal to your tier. You must touch the object to affect it. If the GM feels it appropriate to the circumstances, you can disintegrate a portion of an object (the total volume of which is smaller than you) rather than the entire thing. Action.

SIXTH-TIER PARADOX

Freeze Time (9 Intellect points): You cause time to stop flowing everywhere within immediate range for one minute. The effect ends if you leave the area or if you use an action to end it early. The freezing affects everything in the area except you. Affected creatures are frozen in the moment when you used this revision, and when the effect ends, they resume what they were doing as if no time had passed. Affected creatures and objects are impervious to all damage and cannot be moved or manipulated. You and everything outside the area act normally. Action to initiate.

Recursion Walk (9 Intellect points): When you initiate a translation, instead of translating into a known recursion, you can attempt to translate into a recursion you're not directly familiar with, but one that you specify the general parameters

Hell Frozen Over, page 251

Warded locations, page 129

Translation Failure table, page 128

for. The GM determines the actual nature and characteristics of the recursion you translate to if you are successful. The translation roll is one step more difficult than translating to a recursion of a given level would normally be, plus any additional steps the GM believes is appropriate. For instance, if you specify that you're looking for an Earthlike recursion where your favorite paranormal investigator runs a wizard shop, the difficulty would be 5 (Earth is a level 5 recursion), plus 1 for attempting to find it blind, plus 1 because of the very specific nature of the request, for a total difficulty of 7. Otherwise, normal rules for translation apply. Four hours to initiate; two hours to initiate if hastened by another character; ten minutes to initiate if hastened by another character who's a spinner.

SPINNER: NEW TWISTS

Spinners can add these new special abilities to the list of options when selecting their twists for each tier.

FIRST·TIER SPINNER

Aggression (2 Intellect points): Your words twist the mind of a character within short range who is able to understand you, unlocking her more primitive instincts. As a result, she gains an asset on her Might-based attack rolls for one minute. Action to initiate.

Erase Memories (3 Intellect points): Your words twist the mind of a target within immediate range who is able to understand you, erasing up to the last five minutes of its memory. The target forgets what it experienced during that time. Action.

Terrifying Presence (2+ Intellect points): You attempt to convince one intelligent target within short range that can understand you that you are its worst nightmare. If you are successful, the target becomes panicked. For as long as you do nothing but speak (you can't even move), the target is paralyzed with fear, runs away, or takes some other action appropriate to the circumstances. The target must be level 3 or less. Instead of applying Effort to decrease the difficulty of the roll, you can apply Effort to increase the maximum level of the target. Thus, to terrorize a level 5 target (two levels above the normal limit), you must apply two levels of Effort. Action.

SECOND·TIER SPINNER

Get Away (2 Speed points): After your action on your turn, you move up to a short distance or get behind or beneath cover within immediate range. Enabler.

Speed Recovery (3 Intellect points): Your words enhance the normal regenerative ability of a character within short range who is able to understand you, so that when he makes a recovery roll, he must spend only half the normal amount of time required to do so (minimum one action). Action.

Unexpected Betrayal: Within a round or two of successfully using Enthrall, Fast Talk, or a similar, higher-tier twist on a target within short range, the difficulty of the first attack you make on that target is decreased by two steps. Once you use Unexpected Betrayal on a target, the difficulty for you to use your spinner twists or attempt simple persuasion on that same target is permanently increased by two steps. Enabler.

THIRD·TIER SPINNER

Accelerate (4+ Intellect points): Your words imbue the spirit of a character within immediate range who is able to understand you, accelerating her so that she gains an asset on initiative tasks and Speed defense rolls for 10 minutes. Instead of applying Effort to decrease the difficulty, you can apply Effort to affect more targets, with each level of Effort affecting one additional target. You must speak to additional targets to accelerate them, one target per round. Action per target to initiate.

Discerning Mind: You have +3 to Armor against damaging attacks and damaging effects that

Recovery roll, page 108

Enthrall, page 39

Fast Talk, page 39

A spinner with Discerning Mind has practiced swaying the minds of others so much that she's gained a measure of protection against others attempting the same on her.

target your mind and Intellect. The difficulty of defense rolls you make against attacks that attempt to confuse, persuade, frighten, or otherwise influence you is decreased by one step. Enabler.

Wrest From Chance: If you roll a natural 1 on a d20, you can choose to reroll the die. If you reroll, you avoid a GM intrusion—unless you roll a second 1—and might even succeed on your task. Once you use this twist, it is not available again until after you make a ten-hour recovery roll. Enabler.

FOURTH·TIER SPINNER

Body Memory (4+ Intellect points): You touch and talk to the (mostly complete) corpse of a level 1 or 2 creature, using words infused with quickened energy of the Strange, and the creature stirs back to life for one minute. This is a difficulty 2 Intellect roll. Body Memory works on a given corpse only once. Instead of applying Effort to decrease the difficulty, you can apply Effort to increase the maximum level of the target. Thus, to rouse a level 5 target (three levels above the normal limit), you must apply three levels of Effort. Action.

Expert: Instead of rolling a d20, you can choose to automatically succeed on a task you're trained in. The task must be difficulty 4 or lower, and it can't be an attack roll or a defense roll. Enabler.

Spin Psychosis (4 Intellect points): Your words inflict a destructive psychosis in the mind of a target within long range that can understand you, dealing 6 points of Intellect damage (ignores Armor) per round. The psychosis can be dispersed if a target spends an action calming and centering itself (and doing nothing else). Action to initiate.

FIFTH·TIER SPINNER

Font of Inspiration: With your approval, characters within immediate range can gain inspiration from your presence as an action; the difficulty of one action taken in the following round by an affected character is reduced by one step. This inspiration costs the character 2 Intellect points. Once this twist is used, others

can't gain inspiration from you again until after you make a recovery roll. Enabler.

Foul Aura (5+ Intellect points): Your touch invests an object no larger than yourself with an invisible, psychic short-range aura of doom, fear, and doubt for one day. Creatures of a particular kind that you specify (humans, dragons, kray, and so on) feel an urge to move at least a short distance away from the object. If a creature does not move away, the difficulty of all tasks, attacks, and defenses it attempts while within the aura is increased by one step. The duration of the aura is extended by one day per level of Effort applied. The aura is temporarily blocked while the object is covered or contained. Action to initiate.

Stimulate (6 Intellect points): Your words encourage a target you touch who can understand you. The difficulty of the next action taken by the target is decreased by three steps. Action.

SIXTH·TIER SPINNER

Shatter Mind (7+ Intellect points): Your words reverberate destructively in the brain of an intelligent level 1 target within short range that can understand you. They destroy tissue, memories, and personality, thus triggering a vegetative state. Instead of applying Effort to decrease the difficulty of the attack, you can apply Effort to increase the maximum level of the target. Thus, to shatter the mind of a level 5 target (four levels above the normal limit), you must apply four levels of Effort. Action.

Spinner's Luck: If you fail on a task (including an attack roll or a defense roll), you can change the die result to a natural 20. This still might not be enough to allow you to succeed if the difficulty remains higher than 6. Once you use this twist, it is not available again until after you make a ten-hour recovery roll. Enabler.

Luck is not the chaotic ocean of random chance most people believe it to be, at least not for someone with Spinner's Luck. That said, Spinner's Luck doesn't work if a spinner rolls a natural 1 for an attempted task, unless she also has and uses the third-tier spinner twist Wrest From Chance.

A character can't apply Effort to any task he accomplishes using the Expert twist.

The vegetative state created by Shatter Mind can be healed in recursions that employ advanced Magic or Mad Science, or by a condition remover cypher that cures psychosis.

Condition remover, page 314

DESCRIPTORS

Your character's descriptor influences everything about your character. For example, a Paranoid spinner probably approaches a problem differently than a Brash spinner does. The descriptor changes the way a character goes about every action. It places your character in the situation (the first adventure, which starts the campaign) and helps provide motivation. It is the adjective of the sentence "I am an *adjective noun* who *verbs*."

The descriptors in this chapter expand on those provided in chapter 5 of *The Strange* corebook. However, unlike the descriptors in the corebook, some of the descriptors here are negative in connotation. Addicted, Paranoid, and Slacker, for example, are not terms that most people would want to use to describe themselves. But sometimes a character is better defined by something less than flattering,

possibly because the negative trait is the most remarkable one. Like all descriptors, these have been created to help shape characters and serve as roleplaying prompts. Despite the less-than-positive nature of these particular descriptors, overall, they are equal in what they offer a character. In other words, the positive aspects of being Paranoid make it a "balanced" choice. The point is to create the character you really want to play, have fun, and not pay a steep price for doing it.

Descriptors offer a one-time package of extra abilities, skills, or modifications to your stat Pools. Some descriptors have inabilities— tasks that a character isn't good at. You can think of inabilities as "negative skills"— instead of being one step better at that kind of task, you're one step worse. If you become skilled at a task that you have an inability with, they

Brash, page 46

Addicted, page 16

Paranoid, page 21

Slacker, page 24

GENERAL DESCRIPTORS

Addicted	Fast*	Lucky*	Resolute	Strong*
Appealing*	Graceful*	Materialistic	Sharp-Eyed*	Tough*
Brash*	Intelligent*	Meticulous	Skeptical*	Unforgiving
Clever*	Introverted	Paranoid	Slacker	Virtuous
Crazy	Jovial	Patient	Spiritual	
Creative	Kind	Poker-Faced	Stealthy*	*Descriptors marked with asterisks appear in *The Strange* corebook.
Extroverted	Know-It-All	Resilient	Strange*	

cancel out. Remember that characters are defined as much by what they're *not* good at as by what they *are* good at.

Descriptors also offer a few brief suggestions of how your character got involved with the rest of the group on the first adventure. You can use these, or not, as you wish. In many cases, it's possible you ended up getting involved with the PCs because you were assigned a mission by the Estate, OSR, the Quiet Cabal, or some other organization aware of the nature of the Strange.

You can pick any descriptor you wish regardless of whether you're a vector, a paradox, or a spinner.

The Estate, page 148

OSR, page 157

Quiet Cabal, page 153

Vector, page 25

Paradox, page 30

Spinner, page 38

NEW DESCRIPTORS

When making a new character, you can choose one of these new descriptors.

ADDICTED

You're addicted to a stimulant that provides a brief, amphetamine-like high. You can't break the cycle. Every time you think you've stopped, a few days later you end up putting a spike into your vein, dropping dust in your eye, or self-administering in some other fashion. Whether it's old jack, the white, spiral dust, or some other exciting-sounding name for a dangerous drug, the result is the same. At that point, you don't care about anything but your next fix.

You gain the following characteristics:

Twitchy: +2 to your Speed Pool.

Skill: You are excitable. You are trained in initiative.

Know Where to Score: You are trained in tasks related to maintaining your drug supply.

Drug Consequences: When you take your drug, you can spend an action to gain 4 points you can add to any Pool (even if that Pool is already at its normal maximum, or if no points otherwise remain in that Pool). Immediately after you add points to a Pool, the difficulty of the next task you attempt is decreased by one step. However, until you expend those 4 points from your Pool (or lose them from damage), the difficulty of all subsequent tasks is increased by one step. Though you can use your drug again at any time, you don't gain the advantages described above until after you make a ten-hour recovery roll. In addition, in the hour after you take your drug, GM intrusions appropriate for you include becoming confused and attacking an ally for a couple of rounds, falling unconscious unexpectedly, and getting lost as you travel. You do not earn XP for such GM intrusions.

Initial Link to the Starting Adventure: From the following list of options, choose how you became involved in the first adventure.

1. You were so high you didn't know what you were agreeing to.

2. One of the other PCs gave you money (which you used to buy more of your drug, regardless of what you said you would do with it), and now you're repaying that obligation by helping him with the task at hand.

3. You got on the bad side of a drug dealer. To get away, you joined the other PCs.

4. You think that if you go along on the adventure, you can find a new source for your drug.

CRAZY

You're a risk-taker, you don't think twice about danger, and sometimes, you lose the thread of what's happening around you. You might not have always been like this—that head injury you received that one time might be the root cause. Or maybe your injury just let the real you come out and play. Who cares? During your cognizant periods, you're aware that most others aren't like you, so you might attempt to hold yourself back when in their presence. After all, you don't want them to think you're crazy. But you are. You're a freakin' lunatic, insane in the membrane, and all that jazz, man. Do you catch the frequency? What? Where am I?

You gain the following characteristics:

Crazed Intuition: +2 to your Intellect Pool.

Hyper: +2 to your Speed Pool.

Skill: Your perception of physical pain is blunted. You are trained in Might defense actions.

Erratic Behavior: You are prone to acting erratically or irrationally. When you are in the presence of major phenomena related to the Strange or subjected to great stress (such as a serious physical threat), the GM can use GM intrusion to direct your next action without awarding XP. You can still pay 1 XP to refuse the intrusion. The GM's influence is the manifestation of your madness and thus is always something you would not likely do otherwise, but it is not directly, obviously harmful to you unless there are extenuating circumstances. For example, if a foe suddenly leaps out of the darkness, you might spend the first round babbling incoherently or screaming the name of your pet rat—which is crazy, since you don't have a pet rat.

Inability: Your mind is quite fragile. Whenever you try to resist a mental attack, the difficulty is increased by one step.

Initial Link to the Starting Adventure: From the following list of options, choose how you became involved in the first adventure.

1. One of the other PCs recruited you while you were in one of your lucid phases, before realizing how crazy you actually were.

2. You have reason to believe that being with the other PCs will help you find a cure for what ails you—if not in this recursion, then in some other.

3. You checked yourself out of an institution where you were "vacationing" and joined the PCs to make good your escape.

4. One of the other PCs invited you, but you wonder if it was out of pity.

CREATIVE

Maybe you have a notebook where you write down ideas so you can develop them later. Perhaps you email yourself ideas that strike you out of the blue so you can sort them in an electronic document. Or maybe you just sit down, stare at your screen and, by indomitable

"It is the tension between creativity and skepticism that has produced the stunning and unexpected findings of science."
~Carl Sagan

SWITCHING DESCRIPTORS AFTER CHARACTER CREATION

As the campaign progresses, a player might want to switch the descriptor that she chose when creating her character. As with everything, switching descriptors should be worked out between the player and the GM. The best play experiences come from good communication. If the GM agrees to the change, it should occur because something happens in the game to change the character or because her focus changes due to a new opportunity that arose in the course of play. If you just want to change for the sake of variety or to become more powerful, the GM is unlikely to allow it and may ask you to make a new character instead.

Changing a descriptor is both easy and appropriate, particularly with some of the new descriptors found in this book. For example, in the course of play, a Kind vector's sister is killed by an agent of the Betrayer. The vector swears vengeance, and this justifies changing his descriptor to Unforgiving. On the other hand, if the vector falls on hard times and tries to lose himself in alcohol or drugs, he could change his descriptor to Addicted.

If a switch occurs, the character loses his old descriptor and its benefits. That should be part of the story, too. A Kind vector is no longer concerned about being helpful to others—now he's focused almost entirely on his own vengeance (or erasing the world with drugs).

There's no limitation on the number of times a character can change his descriptor. For example, if the vector finally gets satisfaction, maybe he goes back to being Kind—as long as it fits the story.

force of will, produce something from nothing. However your gift works, you're creative—you code, write, compose, sculpt, design, direct, or otherwise create narratives that enthrall other people with your vision.

You gain the following characteristics:

Inventive: +2 to your Intellect Pool.

Original: You're always coming up with something new. You're trained in any task related to creating a narrative (such as a story, play, or scenario). This includes deception, if the deception involves a narrative you're able to tell.

Skill: You are naturally inventive. You are trained in one specific creative skill of your choice: writing, computer coding, music composition, and so on.

Skill: You love solving riddles and the like. You are trained in puzzle-solving tasks.

Skill: To be creative requires that you always be learning. You are trained in any task that involves learning something new, such as when you're digging through a library, data bank, news archive, or similar collection of knowledge.

Inability: You're inventive but not charming. The difficulty of all tasks related to pleasant social interaction is one step higher for you.

Initial Link to the Starting Adventure: From the following list of options, choose how you became involved in the first adventure.

1. You were doing research for a project and convinced the PCs to bring you along.

2. You're looking for new markets for the results of your creative output.

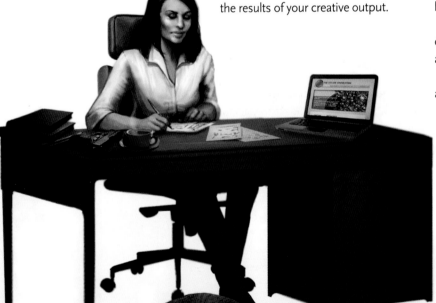

3. You fell in with the wrong crowd, but they grew on you.

4. A creative life is often one beset with financial hurdles. You joined the PCs because you hoped it would be profitable.

EXTROVERTED

You get a charge of emotional energy from being around other people. That means you're outgoing and friendly because otherwise people wouldn't want to be around you. On the other hand, if you find yourself alone for any appreciable amount of time, you hate it. You're at your best sketching out ideas in a room full of other people because you think best while talking. A brainstorm session filled with other people is a bit like nirvana.

You gain the following characteristics:

Animated: +4 to your Speed Pool.

Skill: You're friendly. You're trained in all tasks related to pleasant social interaction and putting other people at ease.

Skill: You're something of a social expert. You're trained in one specific social skill of your choice: dancing, karaoke, a team sport, wine tasting, playing tabletop games, and so on.

Inability: While you are alone, the difficulty of all tasks related to figuring out puzzles or problems, memorizing things, or using lore is increased by one step.

Initial Link to the Starting Adventure: From the following list of options, choose how you became involved in the first adventure.

1. Even though you didn't know most of the other PCs beforehand, you invited yourself along on their outing.

2. You won a bet, and your reward was being asked to help out with an important task.

3. You're pretty sure the PCs will fail without you.

4. Someone said something about a party, and you misunderstood. By then, it was too late.

INTROVERTED

You're at your best by yourself or in a small group of close friends. Being around other people, especially strangers, is tiresome. You can do it; you're not shy or anxious about being around other people, and you can "turn it on" when needed. But after a while, you need to retreat and recharge your emotional energy. When you're alone, you can think, explore your inner mind, and reflect on problems that need a solution.

You gain the following characteristics:

Introspective: +4 to your Intellect Pool.

Deep Thinker: While you are alone, the difficulty of all tasks related to figuring out puzzles or problems, memorizing things, or using lore is decreased by one step.

Cautious: You're trained in Intellect defense actions.

Inability: After you've been in a large group for more than an hour without at least an hour by yourself, the difficulty of all tasks related to pleasant social interaction is increased by one step.

Initial Link to the Starting Adventure: From the following list of options, choose how you became involved in the first adventure.

1. Against your initial inclination, you accepted an invitation to join the team.

2. You lost a bet, and your penalty was being asked to help out with an important task.

3. The solution to a problem came to you, and it was so elegant that you had to share it, even though that meant joining the other PCs.

4. You have to repay a favor, and the adventure offers you a way to do so.

JOVIAL

You're cheerful, friendly, and outgoing. You put others at ease with a big smile and a joke, possibly one at your own expense, though lightly ribbing your companions who can take it is also one of your favorite pastimes. Sometimes people say you never take anything seriously. That's not true, of course, but you have learned that to dwell on the bad too long quickly robs the world of joy. You've always got a new joke in your back pocket because you collect them like some people collect bottles of wine.

You gain the following characteristics:

Witty: +2 to your Intellect Pool.

Skill: You're convivial and set most people at ease with your attitude. You are trained in all tasks related to pleasant social interaction.

Skill: You have an advantage in figuring out the punch lines of jokes you've never heard before. You are trained in all tasks related to solving puzzles and riddles.

Initial Link to the Starting Adventure: From

the following list of options, choose how you became involved in the first adventure.

1. You solved a riddle before realizing that answering it would launch you into the adventure.

2. The other PCs thought you'd bring some much-needed levity to the team.

3. You decided that all fun and no work was not the best way to get through life, so you joined up with the PCs.

4. It was either go with the PCs or face up to a circumstance that was anything but jovial.

KIND

It's always been easy for you to see things from the point of view of other people. That ability has made you sympathetic to what they really want or need. From your perspective, you're just applying the old proverb that "it's easier to catch flies with honey than with vinegar," but others simply see your behavior as kindness. Of course, being kind takes time, and yours is limited. You've learned that a small fraction of people don't deserve your time or kindness—true sadists, narcissists, and similar folk will only waste your energy. So you deal with them swiftly, saving your kindness for those who deserve it and can benefit from your attention.

You gain the following characteristics:

Emotionally Intuitive: +2 to your Intellect Pool.

Skill: You know what it's like to go a mile in someone else's shoes. You're trained in all tasks related to pleasant social interaction and discerning the dispositions of others.

Karma: Sometimes, strangers just help you out. To gain the aid of a stranger, you must pay 1 XP to the GM, and the GM determines the nature of the aid you gain. Usually, the act of kindness isn't enough to turn a bad situation completely around, but it may moderate a bad situation and lead to new opportunities. For example, if you are captured, a guard loosens your bonds slightly, brings you water, or delivers a message.

Inability: Being kind comes with a few risks. The difficulty of all tasks related to detecting falsehoods in the speech and mannerisms of other creatures is increased by one step.

Initial Link to the Starting Adventure: From the following list of options, choose how you became involved in the first adventure.

1. A PC needed your help, and you agreed to come along and add your expertise.

"Your visions will become clear only when you can look into your own heart. Who looks outside, dreams; who looks inside, awakes."
~C.G. Jung

"I learned that it is the weak who are cruel, and that gentleness is to be expected only from the strong."
~Leo Rosten

"They can beg
and they can plead
But they can't see the light,
that's right, that's right
'Cause the boy with the
cold hard cash
Is always Mister Right."
~Madonna

2. You gave the wrong person access to your money, and now you need to make some back.

3. You're ready to take your benevolence on the road and help more people than you could if you didn't join the PCs.

4. Your job, which seemed like it would be personally rewarding, is the opposite. You join the PCs to escape the drudgery.

KNOW·IT·ALL

You never forget anything, though people occasionally accuse you of being resistant to learning new information, especially information that risks upsetting one of your cherished ideals or loudly proclaimed opinions. What other people don't know is that you've already got it all figured out. The secret is watching out for *numero uno*. That said, the people you trust most are also people you sometimes listen to. Even if you don't agree with your friends, you're big enough to let them have the spotlight . . . sometimes.

You gain the following characteristics:

Self-Assured: +2 to your Intellect Pool.

Skill: You rarely forget anything. You are trained in all tasks related to memory and calling up pieces of trivia.

Save Yourself: You're first to the exit in a fire or other disaster, going so far as pushing an ally out of the way to save yourself. When applying Effort to make a defense roll, you can use points from the appropriate Pool of an ally next to you if the ally allows it. Enabler.

Inability: The difficulty of tasks you attempt related to research or learning new information is increased by one step.

Initial Link to the Starting Adventure: From the following list of options, choose how you became involved in the first adventure.

1. You heard the PCs might need an expert, and you showed up to offer your services.

2. The PCs sought you out because one of them is a fan of your earlier work.

3. You're trying to change your ways, and helping the PCs accomplish their task might be just what you need.

4. You believe the only way the PCs will succeed is if you are along to tell them what's what.

MATERIALISTIC

Money is power. Pretending otherwise is stupid, and no one's ever accused you of that. You use your considerable talents to amass cash regardless of your situation. Even if you end up friendless and your capabilities one day fade, a large bank account will be sufficient to buy you new companions, as well as mercenaries to protect your hard-earned assets.

You gain the following characteristics:

Mind for Numbers: +2 to your Intellect Pool.

Skill: You're a haggler. You are trained in all tasks involving the exchange of money.

Skill: You're an accounting whiz. You are trained in studying and retaining knowledge of numbers, patterns, and other minute details.

Midas Presence: Whenever you translate into a recursion, you have 10% more money than when you last visited the recursion.

Inability: Materialistic people are usually a bit unlikeable. The difficulty of all tasks related to pleasant social interaction is one step higher for you.

Initial Link to the Starting Adventure: From the following list of options, choose how you became involved in the first adventure.

1. A banking irregularity led you to the PCs, who showed you something strange.

2. The PCs recruited you because they needed someone with accounting experience.

3. After learning that there's a lot of money in what the PCs intend to do, you asked to be included.

4. Your last business failed (through no fault of your own), and you need some quick cash to avoid going too far in debt.

METICULOUS

You pay attention to details, are scrupulous about everything, and are precise in your words and thoughts. Being careful is its own reward, because those who fail to follow the credo "measure twice, cut once" sometimes don't have the opportunity to make up for their initial mistake. Many organizations have places for someone like you, though sometimes you have a hard time making friends. It's dawned on you that being as hard on other people as you are on yourself might be to blame, so you've added "be nicer" to your list of self-improvement projects, though it keeps slipping to the bottom of the list.

You gain the following characteristics:

Conscientious: +2 to your Intellect Pool.

Skill: You have an eye for detail. You are trained in any task that involves finding or noticing small details.

Skill: Being careful includes improved fine motor control. You are trained in any task that involves manipulating small or delicate objects, working with machinery, or doing similar tasks where a shaking hand could be the difference between success and failure.

Skill: You're hard to fool because your cognizance is more than a tool—it's a shield. You're trained in Intellect defense tasks.

Inability: Your conscientious eye for detail sometimes puts off strangers. The difficulty of any task involving positive social interaction is increased by one step.

Initial Link to the Starting Adventure: From the following list of options, choose how you became involved in the first adventure.

1. Your analysis of a mystery related to something you were working on led you to the PCs.

2. A PC who knew you figured you'd be useful on the mission and asked you along.

3. Assisting the PCs might also help you clear up an issue you've been attempting to take care of.

4. You join the PCs to escape a bad situation.

PARANOID

You're not the trusting sort. You keep an eye out for your enemies, which include all the people who've done you wrong before, but just as important, you look for the ones that you suspect are out there, watching you, waiting for you to slip up, or maybe waiting until you're alone or vulnerable. Of course, you know there's such a thing as paranoid personality disorder, and you try to stay on the sane side of that line. If you do say so yourself, you're mostly successful. But like the popular expression says, "Just because you're paranoid doesn't mean they aren't after you."

You gain the following characteristics:

Quick: +2 to your Speed Pool.

Skill: You've always got at least one eye on your surroundings. You're trained in all tasks involving identifying or assessing danger.

"I'm not a paranoid deranged millionaire."
~Howard Hughes

Skill: You're always ready to flee, resist, or fight back. You're trained in Intellect defense tasks to resist mental effects.

It's Them! You are prone to seeing threats that aren't there. When you are in the presence of major phenomena related to the Strange or subjected to great stress (such as a serious physical threat), the GM can use GM intrusion to direct your next action without awarding XP. You can still pay 1 XP to refuse the intrusion. The GM's influence is your paranoia taking over and thus is always something you would not likely do otherwise. It may have a negative impact on your allies, though it isn't usually directly harmful. For example, you might suddenly become unduly suspicious of a friend—not so much as to attack her outright, but enough to avoid coming to her aid while she is under attack by a third party.

Initial Link to the Starting Adventure: From the following list of options, choose how you became involved in the first adventure.

1. They didn't want you to join the PCs, so you did it to spite them.

2. The PCs offered you a way to help control your condition through action.

3. One or more of the PCs are among the few people you trust—who else would you hang out with?

4. You suspect that if you continue to stay at home alone, they will finally get you.

PATIENT

Being patient might seem to others like a skill you're born with. And to some extent, that's true. But being patient also comes from hard experience and learning from mistakes. You know all too well that allowing yourself to give in to anger or frustration, or acting in the moment rather than planning ahead, rarely leads to ideal outcomes whether you're dealing with people, creatures, or seemingly impossible situations. It's hardest to be patient when your ego is bruised, but even then, you try to remain calm and work out the best solution.

You gain the following characteristics:

Think It Through: +3 to your Intellect Pool.

Skill: Patience is a positive social trait. You're trained in tasks related to persuasion.

Skill: Patience builds mental muscle. You're trained in Intellect defense actions.

Inability: You don't like to jump right into anything. The difficulty of initiative actions (to determine who goes first in combat) is increased by one step.

Initial Link to the Starting Adventure: From the following list of options, choose how you became involved in the first adventure.

1. After spending some time considering all the ramifications of the issue, you joined the other PCs to be "the voice of reason."

2. You got over an insult (real or accidental) that one of the other PCs inflicted on you and joined the group anyway.

3. You've been holding back most of your life. Every so often, it pays to take a few risks. Even the patient can be patient for only so long.

4. Once, you failed to save a life because you spent too long trying to figure out the best way to proceed. You joined the other PCs to learn how to avoid making the perfect the enemy of the good.

POKER·FACED

You rarely show emotion, especially to strangers. Whether you worked to develop this capacity or keeping your thoughts off your face comes naturally, people have a hard time reading you. Happy, sad, surprised, or enraged—most times, you seem equally inscrutable. The calmness of your face and body could reflect an inner pool of peace that shelters you from the storm of emotion that besets so many others. But sometimes you wonder—is your impassivity also keeping you from joy's storied heights?

You gain the following characteristics:

Dispassionate: +2 to your Intellect Pool.

Skill: You like to keep them guessing. You are trained in all tasks related to concealing your true feelings, thoughts, and knowledge. This extends to being trained in deception tasks.

Skill: You're strong-willed and are trained in resisting mental effects.

Initial Link to the Starting Adventure: From the following list of options, choose how you became involved in the first adventure.

1. Another PC saw how calmly you reacted in a minor emergency and invited you along.

2. Only through experience does one find true inner peace, so you volunteered to go on the adventure.

"One could describe Nicolas as impassive. I prefer to say he's poker-faced. Don't play a game of chance with that man unless you're prepared to lose big."
~Shonai Tenketsu

"Patience is a virtue, and I'm learning patience. It's a tough lesson."
~Elon Musk

3. Living in the moment is part of being impassive, and the adventure began before you realized you'd become part of it.

4. You thought you were signing up for a poker tournament, and then things got strange.

RESILIENT

You can take plenty of punishment, both physically and mentally, and come back for more. It takes a lot to put you down. Neither physical nor mental shocks or damage have a lasting effect. You're tough to faze.

You gain the following characteristics:

Resistant: +2 to your Might Pool, and +2 to your Intellect Pool.

Recover: You can make an extra recovery roll each day. This roll is just one action. So each day, you can make two recovery rolls that each take one action, one roll that takes ten minutes, a fourth roll that takes one hour, and a fifth roll that requires ten hours of rest.

Skill: You're almost unstoppable. You are trained in Might defense tasks.

Skill: You're almost unflappable. You are trained in Intellect defense tasks.

Inability: You're hardy but not necessarily strong. The difficulty of any task involving moving, bending, or breaking things is increased by one step.

Inability: You have a lot of willpower and mental fortitude, but you're not necessarily smart. The difficulty of any task involving knowledge or figuring out problems or puzzles is increased by one step.

Initial Link to the Starting Adventure: From the following list of options, choose how you became involved in the first adventure.

1. You were the only one who walked away from a train crash, and an impressed PC invited you to join the group.

2. Someone asked you to watch over one of the PCs in particular, and you agreed.

3. You lost an arm-wrestling challenge to one of the PCs, and as your payment, you had to help him out.

4. You're hoping the challenge will help you forget some recent pain that threatens to make a mockery of your vaunted mental fortitude.

RESOLUTE

When you set your mind to something, little can stop you. Your friends call you determined and unflappable in the face of adversity. Your detractors call you stubborn and incapable of changing your mind even when a better course of action becomes possible. Stubborn? Maybe. But you try to temper your dogged nature so that it doesn't make you inflexible. Sometimes you even succeed.

You gain the following characteristics:

Relentless: +2 to your Might Pool.

Skill: You're assiduous. It takes more than a simple lie to deflect you from your purpose. You are trained in seeing through lies, deception, and disguise.

"It is only through labor and painful effort, by grim energy and resolute courage, that we move on to better things."
~Theodore Roosevelt

Skill: You're contemplative, taking time with new situations to give them their proper due. The difficulty of all tasks involving attention to detail, concentration, or focused movements is decreased by one step.

Initial Link to the Starting Adventure: From the following list of options, choose how you became involved in the first adventure.

1. Someone did you wrong, and by joining the PCs on the mission, you can put things right.

2. You believe that the PCs will fail without you along to see things through.

3. You started the mission to accomplish a goal, and the PCs joined you.

4. You overheard the other PCs discuss their mission and volunteered your services.

SLACKER

You're young—or, at least, you were once. Most of the time, you're cynical, and when you're not, it's because you really don't care. When you miss work, you feel bad, but you've developed the trick of dismissing that feeling from your mind almost immediately. That explains why you've gone through so many jobs. On the other hand, there always seems to be something else right around the corner. You've screwed up, certainly, but things seem to go your way. Lately, you're trying to turn over a new leaf, but, dude, it's so hard to straighten up and fly right, especially if you have to get out of bed before 10 a.m.

You gain the following characteristics:

Too Smart for Your Own Good: +2 to your Intellect Pool.

Just Lucky: When you roll a natural 1, you can reroll it without spending XP. If you roll a 1 a second time, the GM can use GM intrusion normally.

Inability: You never studied, though you may pretend otherwise. The difficulty of any task that involves knowledge, lore gained by study, or problem solving is increased by one step.

Initial Link to the Starting Adventure: From the following list of options, choose how you became involved in the first adventure.

1. You delivered a wrong package or other item to the PCs as they were discussing their mission, and they took a liking to you.

2. You picked the wrong day to stop sleeping in late and ended up joining the adventure.

3. A relative of yours had information the PCs needed to make their plans.

4. What else were you going to do this week?

SPIRITUAL

A sense of awe washes over you when you appreciate a new facet of your religion or a scientific discipline. When a stranger does something kind for someone he's never met before, it's spiritual. However you meditate—whether by taking in breathtaking scenery, reading a book, or repeating mental syllables in a quiet space—it's spiritual. Your spirituality isn't necessarily about religion, though it could be. The main thing is that you're a person who appreciates and even thrills to the positive aspects of existence, and you may help other people do the same.

You gain the following characteristics:

Meditative: +2 to your Intellect Pool.

Likeable: People and animals just seem to like you. You are trained in all tasks related to pleasant social interaction.

Skill: With maturity comes judgment. You're trained in Intellect defense tasks and all tasks that involve resisting temptation.

Helpful: When you help someone with a task, he adds 1 to his roll (this bonus is in addition to the regular benefits of helping someone).

Inability: When you encounter something novel, you hesitate as you take in all the details. The difficulty of initiative actions (to determine who goes first in combat) is increased by one step.

Initial Link to the Starting Adventure: From the following list of options, choose how you became involved in the first adventure.

1. You heard the PCs would be visiting someplace amazing and wanted to share the experience.

2. You have a message of hope, and going along with the PCs might allow you to get that message across to a larger number of people.

3. The mission involves helping others, and you couldn't say no.

4. You were asked by a different organization to keep tabs on the PCs and help them if they got into trouble.

UNFORGIVING

You've always been stubborn, but more than anything else, you're a champion grudge-

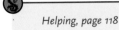

Helping, page 118

holder. If someone does you wrong, you don't forget. That doesn't mean you're single-minded in your need for revenge, just that when the opportunity finally presents itself, you get your payback. On the other hand, you've learned to give your friends some leeway. Not every slight is intentional. But those who knowingly hurt you (or, worse, the people close to you) had better watch out.

If you like, you can work with your GM to come up with an event in your character's past that made you unforgiving. The bad feelings from this event overshadow your other grudges and sometimes appear in your dreams. If you can find resolution one day, maybe you'll no longer be so unforgiving.

You gain the following characteristics:

Battered But Not Beaten: +4 to your Might Pool.

Skill: Payback requires knowing where to find those who've wronged you. You're trained in any task that involves finding and following tracks.

Skill: You may be unforgiving, but that doesn't make you blind to the truth or susceptible to disinformation. You're trained in Intellect defense actions.

Inability: Being unforgiving sometimes makes you a hard person to be around. The difficulty of all tasks related to pleasant social interaction is increased by one step.

Initial Link to the Starting Adventure: From the following list of options, choose how you became involved in the first adventure.

1. The PCs were leaving the area. You invited yourself along to get away from your thoughts.

2. You believe that one of the PCs slighted you. You accompany the group to find out if it was just a misunderstanding on your part.

3. You were lost when the PCs found you, and despite how you expected the strangers to act, they showed you the way out.

4. The PCs accidentally targeted you as the culprit of a major crime. When they realized their mistake, they invited you along to help find the real villain.

VIRTUOUS

Doing the right thing is a way of life. You live by a code, and that code is something you attend to every day. Whenever you slip, you reproach yourself for your weakness and then get right back on track. Your code probably includes

moderation, respect for others, cleanliness, and other characteristics that most people would agree are virtues, while you eschew their opposites: sloth, greed, gluttony, and so on.

You gain the following characteristics:

Dauntless: +2 to your Might Pool.

Skill: You are trained in discerning people's true motives or seeing through lies.

Skill: Your adherence to a strict moral code has hardened your mind against fear, doubt, and outside influence. You are trained in Intellect defense tasks.

Initial Link to the Starting Adventure: From the following list of options, choose how you became involved in the first adventure.

1. The PCs are doing something virtuous, and you're all about that.

2. The PCs are on the road to perdition, and you see it as your task to set them on the proper moral route.

3. One of the other PCs invited you, hearing of your virtuous ways.

4. You put virtue before sense and defended someone's honor in the face of an organization or power far greater than you. You joined the PCs because they offered aid and friendship when, out of fear of reprisals, no one else would.

HERE LIES
LESTER MOORE
FOUR SLUGS
FROM A 44
NO LES
NO MORE

"That's right. I've killed women and children. I've killed just about everything that walks or crawled at one time or another. And I'm here to kill you, Little Bill, for what you did to Ned."
~Will Munny, Unforgiven (1992)

FOCI

Focus, page 51

Your focus is the final twist on your character's type and descriptor. It's the verb of the sentence "I am an *adjective noun* who *verbs*," though the verb has the potential to change with each recursion you translate to, as you take on the context of worlds where Magic, Mad Science, Psionics, or other laws function. The foci presented here supplement those found in *The Strange* corebook. Most are broadly applicable, but some have special rules associated with them. With these new foci, it's easier than ever to ensure that your character remains unique even as you adventure through worlds numberless and strange.

If the character focus you choose is your starting focus, you get a special connection to one or more of your fellow PCs. Your focus also provides a first-tier ability and equipment appropriate to the recursion where the focus is active. Each focus also offers suggestions to

the GM and the player for possible effects or consequences of really good or really bad die rolls.

The more recursions you translate to, the more foci you can potentially accumulate, though usually only one focus is active at a time. Your GM will tell you what foci you can choose from if you're visiting a recursion for the first time and haven't previously selected a focus in that world.

As you progress to a new tier, your active focus grants you more abilities. Each tier's benefit is usually labeled Action or Enabler. If an ability is labeled Action, you must take an action to use it. If an ability is labeled Enabler, it makes other actions better or gives some other benefit, but it's not an action. An ability that allows you to project beams of energy from your eyes is an action. An ability that grants you additional damage against zombies when you make attacks is an enabler. You can use an enabler in the same turn as you perform another action.

The tier benefits of each active focus are independent of and cumulative with benefits from other tiers (unless indicated otherwise). So if your first-tier ability grants you +1 to Armor and your fourth-tier ability also grants you +1 to Armor, when you reach fourth tier, you have a total of +2 to Armor.

STANDARD PHYSICS, MAGIC, AND MAD SCIENCE FOCI

The Foci Table presents three major collections of foci for Earth, Ardeyn, and Ruk. As such, the foci are designed with an eye toward their designated recursion. For instance, Collects Bounties and Serves and Protects are written from the perspective of someone living on Earth, while Rejuvenates the Infirm and Metamorphosizes are written from the perspective of someone native to Ruk.

Every focus, regardless of its listed recursion, could be made available by the GM in alternate recursions that operate under similar laws. Thousands of recursions are seeded around Earth, and many provide a subset of the foci in the Foci Table. Sometimes, a focus fits a new recursion without any fiddling (for example, many Ardeyn foci will work fine in generic fantasy recursions). Other times, some adaptation is required. Consider two different recursion families: "Supers" and "Sci-fi."

SUPERS RECURSIONS
Recursions seeded by comics, anime, and movies about superpowered heroes (the so-called "Supers" recursions) usually operate under the laws of Magic, Mad Science, and Psionics simultaneously. When a character takes a focus offered in a Supers recursion, it's usually because he's taken on the role of a superpowered hero (or villain) in that recursion. The GM could make available foci such as Wears an Iron Suit, Grows to Towering Heights, Throws Boulders, Projects Energy, Masters Wuxia, Soars Across the Sky, and so on. In fact, some of these foci already come with a tier 1 Suit feature. If the GM wants to make a focus available in a Supers recursion that doesn't already have a Suit feature, she can simply add that benefit.

Wears an Iron Suit, page 89

Grows to Towering Heights, page 50

Throws Boulders, page 88

Projects Energy, page 71

Masters Wuxia, page 63

Soars Across the Sky, page 83

●○○ ▬▬▬▬▬▬▬▬▬▬▬▬

TIER 1: SUIT
The tier 1 Suit feature is added to a focus only when the GM wishes to make that focus available in a Supers recursion (and the focus doesn't already have it). The Suit feature grants the character a specially made suit that serves as light armor. The PC is practiced in wearing the suit, so he can wear it for long periods without the usual Might cost per hour or Speed Pool reduction. The suit also usually comes with a utility belt, a mask or helmet, integrated smartphone functionality, and so on. Finally, the suit makes the character look suitably superheroic.

▬▬▬▬▬▬▬▬▬▬▬▬ ●○○

Translates, page 80

 SCI·FI RECURSIONS

Here's another example of adapting one recursion's foci to another recursion. Many recursions, operating under the law of Mad Science (or Mad Science and Psionics), are seeded from movies, novels, and comics that feature spacecraft battles, blaster fights, and rebel heroes. For instance, in a newfound recursion called Rebel Galaxy, the GM should make available Pilots Starcraft, Is a Cyborg, Fires a Blaster, Fights Aliens, Builds Robots, and so on. Most of these require minimal adaptation.

OTHER FOCI

A few of the new foci in this chapter are either too broad or too corner case to be listed directly under Earth, Ardeyn, or Ruk without some adaptation.

Hunts Zombies: This is a specific focus, but one that should be offered in any recursion where zombies roam—the so-called "Zed Omegas." At minimum, both Magic and Mad Science recursions might offer this focus.

Manipulates Strange Energy: Like the Translates focus in the corebook, Manipulates Strange Energy is available to recursors after they've translated at least one time. It's one of a few "meta" foci, and it lets a character interact with the mechanics of the Strange in a way that isn't normally allowed.

Masters Wuxia: This focus is probably available in recursions seeded by the wealth of wuxia films and comics on Earth, in the various "Supers" recursions, and in Ardeyn with some adaptation by the GM and player.

● ○ ○

FOCI TABLE

EARTH (STANDARD PHYSICS)
Calculates the Incalculable (D)
Collects Bounties
Conducts Weird Science*
Entertains* (D)
Excels Physically (D)
Interprets the Law
Is Idolized by Millions
Is Licensed to Carry*
Leads* (D)
Learns Quickly (D)
Looks for Trouble* (D)
Needs No Weapon (D)
Negotiates Matters of Life and Death
Operates Undercover* (D)
Serves and Protects
Solves Mysteries* (D)
Steals (D)
Works the System*

OTHER FOCI
Hunts Zombies
Manipulates Strange Energy (D)
Masters Wuxia
Translates* (D)

ARDEYN (MAGIC)
Abides in Stone*
Awakens Dreams
Carries a Quiver*
Casts Spells
Channels Divine Blessings
Channels Sinfire*
Embraces Qephilim Ancestry*
Goes Berserk
Keeps a Magic Ally
Lives in the Wilderness*
Names
Practices Soul Sorcery*
Shepherds the Dead*
Slays Dragons*
Smites the Wicked
Soars Across the Sky
Speaks for the Land
Throws Boulders
Wields Two Weapons at Once* (D)
Works Miracles*

RUK (MAD SCIENCE)
Adapts to Any Environment* (D)
Aspires to Be Posthuman
Builds Robots
Controls Nanomachines
Fights Aliens
Fires a Blaster
Grows to Towering Heights
Infiltrates*
Integrates Weaponry*
Is a Cyborg
Metamorphosizes*
Pilots Starcraft
Processes Information*
Projects Energy
Regenerates Tissue*
Rejuvenates the Infirm
Resides in Silicon
Sculpts Light
Spawns*
Wears an Iron Suit

PSIONICS
Awakens Dangerous Psychic Talent*

---

*Foci marked with asterisks appear in *The Strange* corebook.

 (D) denotes a draggable focus. A draggable focus may be retained between two recursions, regardless of the law under which the new recursion operates, and even if it does not normally offer that focus to a recursor.

 ● ○ ○

NEW FOCI

ASPIRES TO BE POSTHUMAN

You aspire to become something greater than you are now and personally take the next evolutionary step. In some recursions, such entities already exist. Their abilities so radically exceed those of regular people that they can't really be considered human any longer. You want the same for yourself: to transcend humanity and become posthuman. After you achieve that goal, you'll set your (vastly more powerful) mind to new challenges. Maybe you'll create a recursion of your own or, if you're impatient, modify an existing world to something more to your liking. All you know for sure is that once you transcend, nothing will be beyond your grasp.

You believe in dressing for the job you want, which is why you often wear flowing white robes with simple, elegant lines, made with self-cleaning materials.

Posthuman candidates are usually paradoxes. However, spinners and vectors are also drawn to improving themselves.

Connection: If this is your starting focus, choose one of the following connections.

1. Pick one other PC. You can't seem to affect her with your abilities in any way.

2. Pick one other PC. When that PC holds your hand, you gain +1 to your Intellect Edge.

3. Pick one other PC. You've had a vision that, sometime in the future, she'll be directly responsible for accelerating your posthuman

---

●○○

RULE OF ATTACK SPECIALIZATION

Unless a focus or type ability specifically indicates that you can be specialized in the associated attack, you can't be. Although this might seem like an exception to the general rule that two or more trainings in a task from different sources grant specialization, it's merely an explication of an underlying Cypher System assumption that we've had all along. Focus and type special abilities are designed with this assumption regarding attacks in mind. By calling out this principle as a rule, any potential points of confusion are quashed before they arise.

●○○

---

transcendence, though details are hazy.

4. Pick one other PC. Sometimes when foes attack you and miss, their attacks hit that character instead, and vice versa. It's not something you can consciously control.

Equipment: Clothing appropriate to your recursion (in Ruk, a bodysuit and an umbilical), a silvery metal fragment rumored to be from a posthuman crown in an alternate recursion, a weapon of your choice, and an account with 30 bits.

Posthuman Ability: When you perform moves, revisions, or twists that would normally use force or other energy, they instead use the power of your mind. This alteration changes nothing except the ability's origin.

Minor Effect Suggestion: Your mental ability prevents a foe from moving on its next turn.

Aspires to Be Posthuman GM Intrusions: *A true level 9 posthuman appears and takes an interest in you. An unexpected vision of the future dazes you for a few rounds, but the view is too fragmentary to be anything more than ominous.*

Customizing Foci, page 356

●○○

TIERS ABOVE SIXTH

Getting a character up to the sixth tier will take a long campaign. But what if you want to keep playing the PC after that point? There is no seventh tier. Neither foci nor character types go beyond sixth.

However, you can simulate continued advancement, if you so desire. Allow characters to continue to pay for character benefits (4 XP each) as normal, with the following caveats:

- Do not allow characters to increase their Effort beyond 6. Instead, let them choose another skill or an alternative ability, such as adding 2 to their recovery rolls, reducing the cost of wearing armor, or selecting a new move, twist, or revision.

- Do not allow a character to have an Edge higher than 6 in any one stat.

- When a character gains four benefits, she gains a new tier. At that point, allow her to choose another ability suited to her character type (twists for spinners, revisions for paradoxes, or moves for vectors). Further, allow her to choose any ability (of any tier) from the Customizing Foci ability options in *The Strange* corebook.

●○○

Major Effect Suggestion: Your mental ability breaks a weapon, shield, or piece of armor the target was using.

Tier 1: Move Things With Your Mind (2 Intellect points).

You can manipulate the quantum field to exert force on objects within short range. Once activated, your power has an effective Might Pool of 10, a Might Edge of 1, and an Effort of 2 (approximately equal to the strength of a fit, capable, adult human), and you can use it to move objects, push against objects, and so on, using your own action each time. For example, you could lift and pull a light object anywhere within range to yourself or move a heavy object (like a piece of furniture) about 10 feet (3 m). You could use

Mind Reading revision, page 34

Mind Reading twist, page 42

this power to wield any weapon that you could wield physically (or to make an unarmed attack) with the same training, or lack thereof. You could use this power to lift yourself, but only an immediate distance above solid ground. The power lasts for one hour or until its Might Pool is depleted, whichever comes first. Action.

Tier 2: Improved Mind.
You add 4 points to your Intellect Pool.

Tier 3: Mind Reading (2 Intellect points).
You can read the surface thoughts of a creature within short range, even if the target doesn't want you to. You must be able to see your target. Once you have established contact, you can read the target's thoughts for up to one minute. If you also have the Mind Reading revision or twist, you can use this ability at long range, and you don't need to be able to see the target (but you do have to know that the target is within range). Action to initiate.

Tier 4: Psychic Bolt (3+ Intellect points).
You blast the mind of a target within short range with psychic disruption, inflicting 3 points of damage that ignore Armor. For each 2 additional Intellect points you spend, you can make an Intellect attack roll against an additional target. Action.

Tier 5: Reshape Matter (6 Intellect points).
You can reshape objects on a molecular level. You can affect a single object no larger than you, and the object must be visible and close enough to touch. You can use this ability to damage the object (dealing it 10 points of damage), or you can attempt a crafting task to reshape the object into another form. Reshaping an object usually has a difficulty equal to 1 plus the level of the finished object, and it requires concentrating this power on the object for one minute per level of the finished object. Action to deal damage; one or more minutes to reshape.

Tier 6: Higher State of Existence (6 Intellect points).
You have begun the process of transcending normal matter through fine manipulation of the quantum field. You can change your phase state for up to one minute at a time. When you do, you can't affect or

be affected by normal matter or energy. Only mental attacks and special quantum-field-disrupting energies, devices, or abilities can affect you, but likewise you can't attack, touch, or otherwise affect anything physically.

On the other hand, you can use your mental abilities while phased. Each time you do, there's a chance that the strain causes you to drop out of your phased state (if you roll an odd number on an attack or task roll). If this occurs, you can spend another action to become phased again if the duration of your original phase isn't complete. Action to initiate.

AWAKENS DREAMS

Your dreams are more vivid than other people's. When you dream, those dreams linger on, and when the time is right, you can loose them into reality to impress, confuse, or scare other creatures. You've learned the oneiromancer's craft, which means that you know the secret of lucid dreaming, of gauging the dream state in others, and of mixing herbal elixirs that bring about a restful, dream-filled sleep.

Your clothing probably reflects the eclectic dreamland where you spend so much of your time, including several layers, bright silk ribbons, and odd symbols that made sense when you were dreaming them.

Spinners and paradoxes are most likely to explore the land of dreams.

Connection: If this is your starting focus, choose one of the following connections.

1. Pick one other PC. That character always recognizes your dreams as illusions free of substance and is not fooled or affected by them.

2. Pick one other PC. You accidentally sent that character into a sleep so deep she didn't wake for three days. Whether she forgives you or not is up to her.

3. Pick one other PC. You are certain that you created him from one of your dreams, even if he doesn't believe it.

4. Pick one other PC. You accidentally glimpsed that character's dreams and learned something that she was trying to keep a secret.

Equipment: Ardeyn clothing (or recursion-appropriate clothing), one weapon of your choice, bound journal, ink, a pouch filled with various needful herbs, and 40 crowns.

Minor Effect Suggestion: The target gets turned around, and its next attack is modified by one step to its detriment.

Major Effect Suggestion: You are refreshed by your dream and recover 4 points to one of your Pools.

Tier 1: Dreamcraft (1 Intellect point). You pull an image from a dream into the waking world and place it somewhere within long range. The dream lasts for up to one minute, and it can be tiny or fill an area an immediate distance in diameter. Though it appears solid, the dream is intangible. The dream (a scene, a creature,

Awakens Dreams GM Intrusions: *A stray dream breaks free and comes after you. You begin sleepwalking. Your dream double tries to replace you. Allies have bad dreams after you use certain abilities.*

or an object) is static unless you spend your action each round animating it. As part of that animation, you could move the dream up to a short distance each round, as long as it remains within long range. If you animate the dream, it can make sound but does not produce odor. Direct physical interaction or sustained interaction with the dream shatters it into dispersing mist. For example, attacking the dream shatters it, as does the strain of keeping up appearances when an NPC moves through a dream scene or engages a dream creature in conversation for more than a couple of rounds. Action to initiate; action to animate.

Oneirochemy. You are trained in tasks related to sleep and mixing natural elixirs to help creatures fall asleep. Enabler.

Nightmare: level 5; health 15; inflicts 5 points of damage

Tier 2: Dream Thief (2 Intellect points). You steal a previous dream from a living creature within short range. The creature loses 2 points of Intellect (ignores Armor), and you learn something the GM chooses to reveal about the creature—its nature, a portion of its plans, a memory, and so on. Action.

Tier 3: Dream Becomes Reality (4 Intellect points). You create a dream object of any shape you can imagine that is your size or smaller, which takes on apparent substance and heft. The object is crude and can have no moving parts, so you can make a sword, a shield, a short ladder, and so on. The dream object has the approximate mass of the real object, if you choose. Your dream objects are as strong as iron, but if you do not remain within long range of them, they function for only one minute before fading away. Action.

Consummate Dreamer. You add 2 points to your Intellect Pool. Enabler.

Tier 4: Daydream (4 Intellect points). You pull someone into a daydream, substituting a dream of your own creation for the target's reality for up to one minute. You can affect a target within long range that you can see, or a target within 10 miles (16 km) that you have hair or skin clippings from. To all outward appearances, an affected target stands (or lies) unmoving. But inside, the substituted reality (or dream within a dream, if the target was

sleeping) is what the target experiences. If the target is under duress, it can attempt another Intellect defense roll each round to break free, though the target may not realize its state. Either the dream unfolds according to a script you prepared when you used this ability, or if you spend your own actions (forcing you into a similar state as the target), you can direct the unfolding dream from round to round. Using this ability on a sleeping target decreases the difficulty of your initial attack by one step. Action to initiate; action to direct per round (if this option is exercised).

Tier 5: Nightmare (5 Intellect points). You pull a horrifying creature from your worst nightmare into the waking world and sic it on your foes. The nightmare persists each round while you spend your action concentrating on it (or until you disperse it or it is destroyed). It has one of the following abilities, which you choose when you call it.

Horrify. Instead of making a normal attack, the nightmare's attack horrifies the target, dropping the target to its knees (or similar appendages). The target takes 3 points of damage that ignore Armor and is dazed for one round, during which time the difficulty of all tasks the target performs is modified by one step to its detriment.

Confusion. Instead of making a normal attack, the nightmare's attack confuses the target for one round. On its next action, the target attacks an ally.

Pustule Eruption. Instead of making a normal attack, the nightmare's attack causes rancid, painful pustules to rise all over the target's skin for one minute. If the target takes a forceful action (such as attacking another creature or moving farther than an immediate distance), the pustules burst, dealing 5 points of damage that ignore Armor.

Tier 6. Chamber of Dreams (8+ Intellect points). You and your allies can step into a chamber of dreams, decorated as you wish, that contains a number of doors. The doors correspond with other locations within the recursion that you have visited or know reasonably well. Stepping through one of the doors delivers you to the desired location. This is a difficulty 2 Intellect-based task (which could be modified upward by the GM if the location is warded). Instead of applying Effort to reduce the difficulty, you can apply Effort to key a door to another recursion you've visited (the difficulty of the task is 2 plus the recursion's level). On a success, the door acts as a temporary translation gate, sending you and any allies to wherever you were when you last left that recursion (and you probably lose access to the Awakens Dreams focus in the new recursion). Action to step into chamber of dreams; action to move through a door in the chamber.

BUILDS ROBOTS

Your near-mutant brilliance is mechanically focused, and it allows you to create artificial entities who accept you for who you are. As an added bonus, they do what you command without complaint. You're not entirely sure you've arrived at nirvana by surrounding yourself with artificial beings, but it'll do for now.

Because your robots don't have an opinion, you're not too concerned with your appearance. You tend to throw the same shop coat over whatever you happen to be wearing beneath.

Paradoxes are most drawn to this focus, though sometimes vectors build robots, too, because they appreciate allies in a fight.

Connection: If this is your starting focus, choose one of the following connections.

1. Pick one other PC. Your robotic artificial assistant will take commands from that character as well as from you.

2. Pick one other PC. You created a robot companion for that character, but it promptly tried to kill her, so it had to be destroyed. You're not sure what went wrong.

3. Pick one other PC. You are certain that character is secretly an artificial entity, even if he denies it.

4. Pick one other PC. You created a robotic catlike entity (a level 1 creature) for that character that sometimes shows up but is usually absent pursuing vermin.

Equipment: Clothing appropriate to your recursion (in Ruk, a bodysuit and an umbilical), shop coat, robot spare parts, robot tool kit, weapon of your choice, and an account with 10 bits.

Robot. The word "robot" is used globally in this focus, though the robot you create might look very different from one created by someone else in a different Mad Science recursion. In Ruk, your artificial assistant is a cybernetic chrysalid that incorporates both biological and artificial parts. The nature of the robots you build and can interact with depends on the technology of the recursion; if this focus is offered in a different recursion, robots built there could be primarily metallic, organic, cybernetic, or crystalline, or use some other high technology.

Minor Special Effect: The robot jolts your foe, which modifies any action taken by the foe on its next turn by one step to its detriment.

Major Special Effect: Your robot takes an immediate extra action that you choose.

Builds Robots GM Intrusions: *A robot is hacked. A robot wakes up with a mind of its own. A robot struck in combat unexpectedly detonates. A robot becomes jealous of your living allies.*

Robot assistant: *level 2; health 6; inflicts 2 points of damage*

Improved robot assistant: *level 4; health 12; inflicts 4 points of damage*

Healing, page 116

Tier 1: Robot Assistant. A level 2 robot of your size or smaller (built by you) accompanies you and follows your instructions. You and the GM must work out the details of your robot. You'll probably make rolls for your robot when it takes actions. An assistant robot in combat usually doesn't make separate attacks but helps with yours. On your action, if the artificial assistant is next to you, it serves as an asset for one attack you make on your turn. If the robot is destroyed, you can repair the original with a few days' worth of tinkering, or build a new one with a week's worth of half-time labor. Enabler.

Robot Builder. You are trained in tasks related to building and repairing robots. For the purposes of repair, you can use this skill to heal robots that use similar technology. Enabler.

Tier 2: Robot Control (2+ Intellect points). You use your knowledge of robot command and control (and possibly devices that transmit on the proper frequency) to affect any mechanized system or robot of level 2 or less within short range. You can render several targets inactive for as long as you focus all your attention on them. If you focus on just one target, you can attempt to take active control of it for one minute, commanding it to do simple tasks on your behalf while you concentrate. Instead of applying Effort to decrease the difficulty, you can apply Effort to increase the maximum level of the mechanized system or robot. Thus, to affect a level 4 target (two levels

above the normal limit), you must apply two levels of Effort. Action to initiate.

Tier 3: Robot Improvement. Your artificial assistant increases to level 4. Enabler.

Tier 4: Robot Upgrade. You modify your artificial assistant with one new capability. Standard options include the following. Work with your GM if you prefer a different capability.

Flight. The robot can fly a long distance each round. It can carry you, but only for up to an hour between each of your ten-hour recovery rolls. Enabler.

Cypher Pod. The robot can carry one extra cypher for you. Enabler.

Force Shield. The robot can erect an opaque level 5 force field around itself and anyone within 10 feet (3 m) of it for one minute (or until it is destroyed). It cannot do so again until after your next recovery roll. Action.

Mounted Laser Configuration. The robot can reconfigure itself and become an immobile laser weapon on a gimbal mount. In this configuration, the robot is a heavy weapon that deals 7 points of damage. If the robot acts as an autonomous turret, treat it as a level 3 creature instead of level 4. However, if the laser is fired by you or someone else who has your permission, the difficulty of the laser attacks is decreased by one step. Action to reconfigure; action to return to normal robot configuration.

Tier 5: Robot Fleet. You can choose another upgrade from tier 4, or you can take Robot Fleet. If you take Robot Fleet, you build up to four level 2 robot assistants, each no larger than yourself. (They are in addition to the assistant you built at first tier, which has seen a few upgrades since then.) You and the GM must work out the details of these additional robots. If a robot is destroyed, you can build a new one (or repair the old one from its parts) after a week of half-time labor. Enabler.

Tier 6: Robot Evolution. You can choose another upgrade from tier 4, or you can take Robot Evolution. If you take Robot Evolution, your first artificial assistant increases to level 5, and each of your level 2 robots increases to level 3. Enabler.

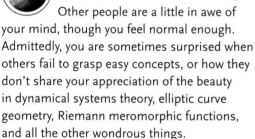

CALCULATES THE INCALCULABLE

Other people are a little in awe of your mind, though you feel normal enough. Admittedly, you are sometimes surprised when others fail to grasp easy concepts, or how they don't share your appreciation of the beauty in dynamical systems theory, elliptic curve geometry, Riemann meromorphic functions, and all the other wondrous things.

You live a little too much in your head to concern yourself with how you look. Your hair is probably slightly too long and tousled, your clothing is casual and stained with coffee, and your socks don't match.

Connection: If this is your starting focus, choose one of the following connections.

1. Pick one other PC. If it wasn't for you, this character never would have passed his college math requirements.

2. Pick one other PC. She seems strangely interested in your mathematical skills. It's up to her whether she is fascinated or disturbed by them.

3. Pick one other PC. Based on a couple of comments you've overheard, you suspect that this character doesn't hold math in the highest regard.

4. Pick one other PC. The character seems to be a variable that never quite solves the same way twice when you include him in an equation, but you haven't the slightest idea why.

Equipment: Street clothes, chalk, laptop, eyeglasses, either a Fields Medal (recognizing your achievements in math) or one weapon of your choice, smartphone, $45.

Minor Effect Suggestion: You don't have to spend an action observing to make your next predictive equation or predictive model.

Major Effect Suggestion: Intuition flares, and you can ask the GM one question about what you're looking at.

Tier 1: Predictive Equation (2 Intellect points). You observe or study a creature, object, or location for at least one round. The next time you interact with that creature or object (possibly in the following round), the difficulty of a related task (such as persuading the creature, attacking it, or defending from its attack) is reduced by one step. If you also have the spinner twist Understanding, one use of either ability reduces the difficulty of two related tasks. Action to observe.

Higher Mathematics. You are trained in standard and higher mathematics.

Tier 2: Predictive Model (2+ Intellect points). If you've used Predictive Equation on a creature, object, or location within the last few days, you can learn one random fact about the subject that is pertinent to a topic you designate. If you

Calculates the Incalculable Equipment:
Ardeyn: *Ardeyn clothing, an abacus, a weapon of your choice, 70 crowns.*
Ruk: *Ruk clothing, an umbilical, a graft that can holographically project calculations as you draw them in thin air, a weapon of your choice, an account with 40 bits.*

Evolved robot assistant: *level 5; health 15; inflicts 5 points of damage*

Understanding, page 40

Calculates the Incalculable GM Intrusions: *Your calculation fails to include pertinent data. Predictive Model reveals how to avoid an attack, but it requires that an adjacent ally be affected instead. You get lost in the beauty of the equations for a round and take no actions.*

Calculates the Incalculable is a draggable focus.

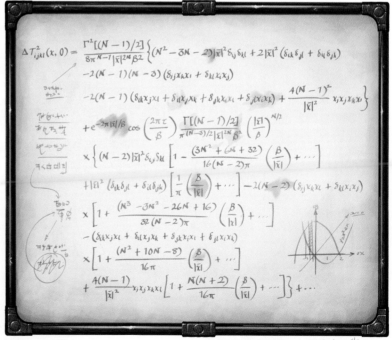

also have the paradox revision Premonition, one use of either ability grants you two random but related facts about the subject. In addition, you can use Predictive Model on the same subject multiple times (even if you've learned a creature's level), but each time you do, you must apply one additional level of Effort than on your previous use. Action.

Tier 3: Subconscious Defense. Your subconscious constantly runs predictive models for avoiding danger. The difficulty of your Speed defense tasks is reduced by one step. Enabler.

Tier 4: Cognizant Offense. During combat, your brain shifts into a sort of battle mode where all potential attacks you could make are plotted on vector graphs in your mind's eye, which always provides the best option. The difficulty of your attacks is reduced by one step. Enabler.

Tier 5: Genius. The more you use your brain, the better it gets. You add 5 points to your Intellect Pool. Enabler.

Further Mathematics. You are specialized in higher mathematics. If you are already specialized, choose some other sphere of knowledge to become trained in. Enabler.

Tier 6: One Step Ahead of Everyone (6 Intellect points). Few things elude your intellectual grasp. Ask the GM one question and get a general answer. The GM assigns a level to the question, so the more obscure the answer, the more difficult the task. Generally, knowledge that you could find by looking somewhere other than your current location is level 1, and obscure knowledge of the past is level 7. Gaining knowledge of the future is impossible, unless you also have the Knowing the Unknown paradox revision, in which case you could predict something that is slated to happen within a day (if you ask the right question). Action.

 CASTS SPELLS
You can cast spells of arcing lightning, rolling fire, creeping shadow, and summoning. As a spellcaster, you understand that the world is a construct built on hidden formulas, flows of energy, and encrypted arcane secrets. Spells are specific flaws in reality that have been identified, studied, and codified into a spellbook for ease of reference and use. Though you likely apprenticed under a more accomplished spellcaster, sorcerer, or wizard, you quickly learned that the most powerful spells—those that can alter a creature's form, open pathways to other worlds, or kill with a single word—are jealously guarded secrets even among friendly spellcasters, including between master and apprentice.

You probably wear sturdy robes stitched with esoteric symbols, carry a staff etched with indecipherable glyphs, and, last but certainly not least, carry a tome of magic spells wherever you go.

Paradoxes and spinners make excellent spellcasters.

Connection: If this is your starting focus, choose one of the following connections.

1. Pick one other PC. You worry that she is trying to get a look at your spellbook, but you don't know why.

2. Pick one other PC. You once accidentally turned him into a tiny, insignificant creature. Though you were unable to revert him, he eventually returned to his normal form.

3. Pick one other PC. That character is related to the spellcaster you apprenticed under.

4. Pick one other PC. Every so often when you cast a spell, that character later reacts as if she had an allergic reaction. She doesn't yet know the cause of her affliction, but you do. You're still debating whether to tell her or let her suffer in ignorance while you work on a spell to assuage her condition.

Equipment: Esoteric robes, quill and ink bottle, spellbook, staff (light or medium weapon), notes taken from another caster's spellbook you've yet to decipher, and 100 crowns.

Spellcasting Special Abilities: If you perform revisions or twists, you do so as spells you cast, which involve an arcane gesture or two, a few mystical words, and possibly a pinch of dust or other material to invoke the effect. (Your revisions and twists appear as spells codified in your spellbook.) This alteration changes nothing other than how you trigger the effects. For example, when a spinner who Casts Spells

Premonition, page 32

Knowing the Unknown, page 37

Casts Spells GM Intrusions: *A spell in your spellbook is defaced and ruined. A summoned creature turns on you regardless of precautions. A rival spellcaster tries to steal your spellbook. A Fire Bloom Spell goes awry and catches one or more allies in its area.*

uses Enthrall, she does so by first making a particular hand gesture and uttering the syllables of the spell, after which her eyes glow with a captivating, enthralling light.

Minor Effect Suggestion: Your spell hazes the target's vision with a magic glow so that all tasks it attempts on its next action are modified by one step to its detriment.

Major Effect Suggestion: A pulse of arcane energy removes the target from reality for a brief period. When the target reappears a couple of rounds later, no time has passed for it.

Tier 1: Spellbook. You've compiled a tome of spells, formulas, and notes that grants you flexibility that other sorcerers don't possess. With your spellbook, you can replace one of your readied spells (such as the Arcane Flare Spell, Magic Shield Spell, Ray of Confusion Spell, and so on) with a different one of the same tier that is also in your spellbook. You can have only one readied spell of a given tier at a time. To make the switch, spend ten minutes studying your spellbook, after which time your readied spell is changed out. A spellcaster can choose to vary her readied spells up to twice per day, immediately after a one-hour or ten-hour recovery roll. (Changing out the spell requires only about a minute.)

Choose one of the following spells as your readied spell for tier 1.

Arcane Flare Spell (1 Intellect point). You enhance the damage of another attack spell (a twist or revision) with an extra charge of energy so that it deals 1 additional point of damage. Alternatively, you attack a target within long range by projecting a flare of raw magic that inflicts 4 points of damage. Enabler for enhancement; action for long-range attack.

Magic Shield Spell (1 Intellect point). You gain +1 to Armor for an hour. Action to initiate.

Tier 2: Spellbook. You add these additional spells to your spellbook. Choose one of the following spells as your readied spell for tier 2.

Ray of Confusion Spell (2 Intellect points). You project a grey beam of confusion at a creature within short range, inflicting 1 point

of damage that ignores Armor. In addition, until the end of the next round, the difficulty of all tasks, attacks, and defenses the target attempts is modified by one step to the target's detriment. Action.

Lock Spell (2+ Intellect points). A door, gate, chest, drawer, locket, or other object that can be closed within long range snaps shut and is magically locked (level 3 effect) for one hour. If an object or creature is physically holding the target object open, you must also succeed on an Intellect-based attack. For each level of Effort you apply, the quality of the magic lock increases by one level. Action to initiate.

Enthrall, page 39

Given how Casts Spells functions, a spellcaster might wonder if other spells exist for each tier besides those presented here. The answer is for the GM to determine. If any did exist, the character would first have to track them down and enter them into her spellbook.

Umber wolf, page 295

Night Vault, page 183

Ardeyn, page 160

Demon of Lotan, page 265

Tier 3: Spellbook. You add these additional spells to your spellbook. Choose one of the following spells as your readied spell for tier 3.

Fire Bloom Spell (4+ Intellect points). Fire blooms within long range, filling an area 10 feet (3 m) in radius and inflicting 3 points of damage on all affected targets. Effort applied to one attack counts for all attacks against targets in the area of the bloom. Even on an unsuccessful attack, a target in the area still takes 1 point of damage. Flammable objects in the area may catch fire. Action.

Summon Umber Wolf Spell (4+ Intellect points). An umber wolf appears within immediate range, plucked from the Night Vault of Ardeyn. If you applied a level of Effort as part of the summoning, the umber wolf is amenable to your instructions; otherwise, it acts according to its nature. Regardless, the creature persists for up to one minute before it fades away. Action to initiate.

Tier 4: Spellbook. You add these additional spells to your spellbook. Choose one of the following spells as your readied spell for tier 4.

Soul Interrogation Spell (5 Intellect points). You determine the weaknesses, vulnerabilities, qualities, and mannerisms of a single creature within long range. The GM should reveal the creature's level, basic abilities, and obvious weaknesses (if any). The difficulty of all actions you attempt that affect that creature—attack, defense, interaction, and so on—is reduced by one step for a few months afterward. Action.

Elemental Protection Spell (4+ Intellect points). You and every target you designate within immediate range gains +5 to Armor against direct damage from one type of elemental damage (such as fire, lightning, shadow, or thorn) for one hour, or until you cast this spell again. Each level of Effort applied increases the elemental protection by +2. Action to initiate.

Tier 5: Spellbook. You add these additional spells to your spellbook. Choose one of the following spells as your readied spell for tier 5.

Dragon's Maw Spell (6 Intellect points). You fashion and control a "hovering" phantasmal construct of magic within long range that resembles a dragon's head. The construct lasts for up to an hour, until it is destroyed, or until you cast another spell. It is a level 4 construct that inflicts 6 points of damage with its bite when directed. While the construct persists, you can use it to manipulate large objects, carry heavy items in its mouth, or attack foes. If you use it to attack foes, you must spend your action directly controlling the phantom maw for each attack. Action to initiate.

Granite Wall Spell (7+ Intellect points). You create a level 6 granite wall within short range. The wall is 1 foot (0.3 m) thick and up to 20 feet by 20 feet (6 m by 6 m) in size. It appears resting on a solid foundation and lasts for about ten hours. If you apply three levels of Effort, the wall is permanent until destroyed naturally. Action to initiate.

Tier 6: Spellbook. You add these additional spells to your spellbook. Choose one of the following spells as your readied spell for tier 6.

Summon Demon of Lotan Spell (7+ Intellect points). A demon of Lotan appears within immediate range, plucked from the Night Vault of Ardeyn. If you applied a level of Effort as part of the summoning, the demon is amenable to your instructions; otherwise, it acts according to its nature.

Regardless, the demon persists for up to one minute before it fades away—you hope. Action to initiate.

Word of Death Spell (7+ Intellect points). Your attack is the utterance of a magic word so terrible that it snuffs the life from a living target within short range. The target must be level 1. Instead of applying Effort to decrease the difficulty, you can apply Effort to increase the maximum level of the target. Thus, to kill a level 5 target (four levels above the normal limit), you must apply four levels of Effort. Action.

CHANNELS DIVINE BLESSINGS

Everything seemed meaningless. With the Maker killed and the Incarnations gone, hope was hard to find. You moved blindly forward on the residual, eroding grace of vanished divine beings. But when things seemed most bleak, you were saved. You pledged yourself to a new purpose. If the Incarnations are gone, their power isn't: divine energy remains infused in the land itself. By acting as a servitor of the vanished Incarnations, you are renewed in purpose and joy. If your actions are pure enough, maybe the Incarnations will one day return.

You wear simple clothes, though you also display the symbols and insignia of the Seven Incarnations. Normally humble, you are strident when speaking with the authority of the divine.

Spinners make ideal channelers, mainly because they're especially adept at preaching the good word to those not initially inclined to care.

Connection: If this is your starting focus, choose one of the following connections.

1. Pick one other PC. You were a drunk or otherwise lost to questionable practices until this character plucked you out of the gutter and cleaned you up. You found your calling after that.

2. Pick one other PC. You're concerned that her spirit is bound for the Heart Core, where Lotan burns.

3. Pick one or more other PCs. You say a prayer for each of them, each day. They may or may not know or care that you are doing so.

4. Pick one other PC. That character has confided in you that he doesn't think the Incarnations will ever return, and if they do, they won't be what you expect. You're not sure how to deal with that.

Equipment: Clothing appropriate to your recursion, light armor, one weapon of your choice, an explorer's pack, a symbol of your faith carved in iron, and 100 crowns.

Minor Effect Suggestion: The power of faith knocks the target back several paces.

Major Effect Suggestion: The power of faith knocks the target prone.

Channels Divine Blessings GM Intrusions: *A spirit, demon, or inimical Stranger's faith overcomes your blessing. An NPC is possessed by a demon. An NPC ally in the faith proves to be corrupt. Your symbol of faith cracks for no apparent reason.*

Maker, page 160

Incarnations, page 162

Heart Core, page 186

Tier 1: Divine Knowledge. You are trained in all tasks related to knowledge of godly beings (which, in Ardeyn, is knowledge relating to the Maker, Lotan, and the Incarnations). Enabler.

Blessing of the Sacred Incarnations. As a servant of the absent Incarnations, you can call up blessings in their name. Choose two Incarnations. You gain the associated two abilities described below.

Commerce. You are trained in detecting the deceptions of other creatures. Enabler.

Death (2+ Intellect points). One level 1 demon, spirit, inimical Stranger, or similar creature within short range is destroyed or banished. Instead of applying Effort to decrease the difficulty, you can apply Effort to increase the maximum level of the target. Thus, to destroy or banish a level 5 target (four levels above the normal limit), you must apply four levels of Effort. Action.

Desire (3 Intellect points). With a touch, you restore 1d6 points to one stat Pool of any creature, including yourself. This ability is a difficulty 2 Intellect task. Each time you attempt to heal the same creature, the task difficulty increases by one step. The difficulty returns to 2 after that creature rests for ten hours. Action.

Law (3 Intellect points). In the name of the Incarnations, you prevent a foe that can hear and understand you from attacking anyone or anything for one round. Action.

Lore (3 Intellect points). Choose up to three creatures (potentially including yourself). For one minute, the difficulty of a particular type of task (but not an attack roll or defense roll) is reduced by one step for those creatures, but only while they remain within immediate range of you. Action.

Silence (3 Intellect points). You create a quiet bubble of protection around you to an immediate radius for one minute. The bubble moves with you. The difficulty of all defense rolls for you and all creatures you designate within the bubble is decreased by one step, and no noise, regardless of its origin, sounds louder than a normal speaking voice. Action to initiate.

War (1 Intellect point). A target you choose within short range (potentially yourself) deals 2 additional points of damage with its next successful weapon attack. Action.

Tier 2: Divine Fortitude. Your faith gives you additional reserves. Add 4 points to your Intellect Pool.

Tier 3: Divine Radiance (2 Intellect points). Your prayer calls divine radiance from the heavens to punish an unworthy target within long range, inflicting 4 points of damage. If the target is a demon, spirit, or inimical Stranger, it also stands in unwilling awe of the divine energy coursing through it and is unable to act on its next turn. Once exposed to this blessing, the target can't be awed by this attack again for several hours. Action.

Tier 4: Overawe (5 Intellect points). A blast of divine radiance from the heavens spotlights a target you select within long range, pushing the target to its knees (or similar appendages, if any) and rendering it helpless in the light for up to ten minutes, or until it breaks free. The overawed target cannot defend itself, make attacks, or attempt anything other than to shake free of the divine awe each round. If the target is a demon, spirit, or inimical Stranger, it also takes 1 point of damage that ignores Armor each round it remains affected. Action to initiate.

Tier 5: Divine Intervention (2 Intellect points, or 2 Intellect Points + 4 XP). You ask the divine to intervene on your behalf, usually against a creature within long range, changing the course of its life in a small way by introducing a major special effect upon it. The major special effect is akin to what occurs when you roll a natural 20 on an attack. If you want to try for a larger effect, and if the GM allows it, you can attempt a divine intervention with a more far-reaching effect, which is more like the kind of GM intrusion initiated by the GM on her players. In this case, Divine Intervention costs 4 XP, the effect may not work out exactly like you hope, and you may not make another plea for divine intervention for a week. Action.

Tier 6: Divine Symbol (5+ Intellect points). You invoke divine power by scribing a glowing symbol of one of the Incarnations in the air with your fingers. Writhing pillars of divine radiance spear up to five targets within long

A Stranger is the term for any creature native to the Strange, rather than Earth or a recursion.

Symbols of Ardeyn's Incarnations:

Commerce: Coin
Death: Skull
Desire: Lips
Law: Balance
Lore: Tome
Silence: Eyes
War: Sword

range. A successful attack on a target inflicts 5 points of damage. If you apply Effort to increase the damage, you deal 2 additional points of damage per level of Effort (instead of 3 points); however, targets take 1 point of damage even if you fail the attack roll. Action.

COLLECTS BOUNTIES

Nothing beats the adrenaline rush when you finally nab someone you've tracked across three counties—except maybe collecting the reward for making the arrest. When someone charged with a crime is released on bail bond money and then skips town, you're the best shot the system has for locating the perpetrator, and making the world a safer place by putting the bad guy back behind bars.

You wear heavy boots, a leather jacket, and an obvious holster for your weapon (whatever it is); concealed weapons are not your gig. You want everyone to know you mean business.

Vectors and spinners are equally likely to be drawn to Collects Bounties.

Connection: If this is your starting focus, choose one of the following connections.

1. Pick one other player character. She (presumably) accidentally provided information to a competing bounty hunter that lost you the reward on what would have been a particularly lucrative arrest.

2. Pick one other PC. You happened to see a few documents online while tracking down something unrelated, which leads you to believe he's not exactly who he says he is. You've since grown more comfortable with him, but you remain vigilant in case he turns out to be dangerous.

3. Pick one other PC. She rescued you from a vehicle accident, pulling you out of the wreckage at great risk to herself.

4. Pick one other PC. He knows a secret story about your past that doesn't reflect especially well on your character. But back then, you were young and stupid, not like today. Right?

Equipment: Durable clothing and boots, Stetson hat, heavy leather trench coat (light armor), two weapons of your choice, a license identifying you as a Bail Enforcement Agent, and $300.

Minor Effect Suggestion: The difficulty of your next attack against the foe is decreased by one step.

Major Effect Suggestion: Make an immediate extra attack on your foe.

Tier 1: Tracker and Hunter. When tracking, looking for, or hiding from living people, the difficulty of the task is decreased by one step. Enabler.

Trained and Licensed. You had to demonstrate a basic level of competence to get your license. That license grants you the legal ability to arrest those who signed a bail bond contract and then skipped their court date. You are trained in all tasks related to knowledge of bail, bonds, and your rights to enforce a bail bond contract even when local police cannot.

When someone signs a bail bond contract, he waives his constitutional rights and agrees that he can be arrested by the bail bond agent.

Collects Bounties GM Intrusions: *Your weapon misfires. Your documents are not in order. You have misidentified your target. A police officer mistakes you for a criminal.*

A "skip" is bounty hunter slang for someone who accepts a bail bond loan and then skips his court date.

Tier 2: Expert Combatant. Choose one type of attack in which you are not already trained: light bashing, light bladed, light ranged, medium bashing, medium bladed, medium ranged, heavy bashing, heavy bladed, or heavy ranged. You are trained in attacks using that type of weapon. Enabler.

Know Where It Hurts. You inflict 2 additional points of damage when fighting living people. Enabler.

Tier 3: Roll With the Punches. Sometimes a "skip" gets rough, and you've got to evade an attack. You are trained in Speed defense tasks. Enabler.

Tier 4: Thinking It Through. Skips with bails set at astronomical levels are the most lucrative bounties. They are also the hardest to track down. Thankfully, street smarts are your secret weapon. You add 4 points to your Intellect Pool. Enabler.

Tier 5: Master Combatant. You deal 2 additional points of damage with one weapon attack that you are trained or specialized in. Enabler.

Tier 6: Knock-out Blow (5+ Might points). These days, bounties are rarely "dead or alive"—to get your commission, you need to bring your target back alive. If you strike a living human target of level 3 or less with a weapon you're trained or specialized in, the target is dazed or rendered unconscious (and can take no actions) for one minute. Instead of applying Effort to decrease the difficulty, you can apply Effort to increase the maximum level of the target. Thus, to knock out a level 6 target (three levels above the normal limit), you must apply three levels of Effort.

CONTROLS NANOMACHINES

You have a natural (or implanted) ability to control a specially developed strain of machines or robots whose components are close to the scale of a nanometer. You can't control all nanomachines—just the ones you have special command over. That doesn't limit you too much, though, because you use your own body as a reservoir. Nanomachines constantly replicate inside you, which gives you the ability to infect others, possibly without them being the wiser. Once you've infected something with nanomachines, you can learn an amazing amount of information about it, harm it, freeze it, siphon its energy, or even meld it to your own body.

You probably wear a cloak with a hood or something similar to hide the sheen of sparkling highlights that covers your nanomachine-infused flesh.

Spinners and paradoxes both enjoy controlling nanomachines.

Connection: If this is your starting focus, choose one of the following connections.

1. Pick one other PC. If that character is next to you and takes no action other than to remain next to you, she learns everything that you learn from areas you infuse with nanomachines.

2. Pick one other PC. You suspect that character is afraid of your nanomachines, though he hasn't said anything overt.

Controls Nanomachines GM Intrusions: *It turns out that all of your allies have been infected with nanomachines. A target of nanomachine infusion gains some measure of control over them. Nanomachines infecting an area reject their programming and begin to grow wild.*

3. Pick one other PC. She is somehow resistant to being infused by nanomachines, and you're fascinated by what it might mean.

4. Pick one other PC. He seems to develop a skin rash in the presence of your nanomachines, and you're not quite sure what to do about it (or even if you should tell him). At this point, you merely hope it doesn't get any worse.

Equipment: Clothing appropriate to your recursion (in Ruk, a bodysuit and an umbilical), a green crystal infused with nanomachines, a weapon of your choice, and an account with 60 bits.

Minor Effect Suggestion: You learn the target's name.

Major Effect Suggestion: The target reacts strongly to being infused with nanomachines and is unable to act for a round while seized with tremors.

Tier 1: Nano Infusion (1+ Intellect point). You infect a location (and everything within it) with thousands of microscopic, invisible nanomachines with a wave of your hand. The area infected is equal in size to a 10-foot (3 m) cube and includes all objects or creatures within that area. The area must be within short range. You can use this ability more than once between ten-hour recovery rolls; however, each time you do, you must spend 1 additional point of Intellect (for instance, if you infect three areas with nanomachines, it would cost you 1, then 2, then finally 3 Intellect points). Each creature within the area can attempt to resist your attack if it chooses, even if it doesn't realize what you're up to (assume creatures that are not allies always resist). Once a creature, location, or object is infected, you thereafter always know the direction and distance to it. Furthermore, you can burn all the infecting nanomachines out of one target within short range as an action, which deals the target 3 points of damage that ignore Armor. Action.

Tier 2: Nano-Assisted Scan (2 Intellect points). If you've previously used Nano Infusion on a creature, location, or object, you can scan it (regardless of how far away from it you are). Scanning a creature or object always reveals its level (a measure of how powerful, dangerous,

or difficult it is). You also learn whatever facts the GM feels are pertinent about the matter and energy in that area. For example, you might learn that the wooden box contains a lithium ion battery connected to a magnetic bottle that contains a massive plasma charge. You might learn that the glass cylinder is full of neurodegenerative gas, and that its metal stand has an electrical field running through it that connects to a metal mesh in the floor. You might learn that the creature standing before you is a mammal with a small brain. However, this ability doesn't tell you what the information means. Thus, in the first example, you don't know what the plasma charge is for. In the second, you don't know if stepping on the floor causes the cylinder to release the gas. In the third, you might suspect that the creature is not very intelligent, but scans, like looks, can be deceiving. Action.

Tier 3: Nano-Assisted Stasis (3 Intellect points). If you've previously used Nano Infusion on a creature, you can surround it with scintillating energy, keeping it from moving or acting for one minute, as if frozen solid. You must be able to see the target, and it must be within short range. While in stasis, the target is impervious to harm, cannot be moved, and is immune to all effects. Action.

Tier 4: Nanosculpt (5 Intellect points). If you've previously used Nano Infusion on an object, you can reshape it. If you spend only one action using Nanosculpt, the changes you make are crude at best. If you spend at least ten minutes and succeed at an appropriate crafting task (with a difficulty at least one step higher than normal, due to the circumstances), you can make complex changes to the material. You can't change the nature of the material, only its shape. Thus, you can make a hole in a wall or floor, or you can seal one up. You can fashion a rudimentary sword from a large piece of iron. You can break or repair a chain. With multiple uses of this ability (as well as additional uses of Nano Infusion), you could bring about large changes, making a bridge, a wall, or a similar structure.

Using this ability on a living creature to modify its shape and appearance without

If an ability functions regardless of how far away you are from the target, that means it also works if you and the target are on different recursions. In this case, the character knows the direction and distance to the nearest translation or inapposite gate that leads to the target's current recursion.

hurting or killing it is normally impossible without hours of preparation and support facilities. Therefore, if you use Nanosculpt on a creature infected with your nanobots, treat it as an attack that deals 5 points of damage that ignore Armor.

One or more actions.

Tier 5: Resorb Energy (7 Intellect points). If you've previously used Nano Infusion on an object, you can attempt to siphon its energy. If you touch a cypher, you render it useless. If you touch an artifact, roll the artifact's depletion chance. If you touch another kind of powered machine or device, the GM determines whether its power is fully drained. In any case, you absorb energy from the object touched and regain 1d10 Intellect points. If this would give you more Intellect than your Pool's maximum, the extra points are lost, and you must make a Might defense roll. The difficulty of the roll is equal to the number of points over your maximum you absorbed. If you fail the roll, you take 5 points of damage and are unable to act for one round. Action.

Tier 6: Meld Cypher. Choose one cypher that you have infected with Nano Infusion. The cypher must have an effect that is not instantaneous. You destroy the cypher and gain its power, which functions for you continuously. You can choose a cypher when you gain this ability, or you can wait and make the choice later. After you usurp a cypher's power, you cannot later switch to a different cypher—the ability works only once. If you also have the paradox revision Usurp Cypher, you can use Meld Cypher one additional time to change out a cypher you've previously melded or usurped. The cypher ability you gain functions in whatever recursion you translate to. Action to initiate.

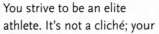

EXCELS PHYSICALLY

You strive to be an elite athlete. It's not a cliché; your body *is* a temple. You glorify it every day with rituals that include a whole food diet, regular hydration, and a regimen of exercise targeting conditioning, strength, and speed. When things

get crazy and the world explodes with chaos and uncertainty, you've still got your body and your health under control.

You likely wear athletic, sweat-wicking clothing—probably branded in some fashion—that doesn't hinder you as you move or work out. If you're not carrying your gym bag with you, it's nearby.

Vectors are made for this focus.

Connection: If this is your starting focus, choose one of the following connections.

1. Pick one other PC. You gave that PC a helping hand when no one else would during a difficult period.

2. Pick one other PC. You are concerned by all the junk food you see this character eat, and you want to say something.

3. Pick one other PC. That character's parent made a popular workout video fifteen years ago that in many ways changed your life.

4. Pick one other PC. She owes you $100.

Equipment: Athletic clothing, spare street clothes, gym bag (with jump rope, towel, hand sanitizer, and so on), membership card for an athletic club, electronic fitness monitoring bracelet, smartphone, $50.

Minor Effect Suggestion: You restore 2 points to your Might Pool.

Major Effect Suggestion: Your foe pauses, impressed by your prowess despite himself, and takes no action on his turn.

Tier 1: Muscled. You add 2 points to your Might Pool. Enabler.

Athlete. You are trained in lifting heavy things, jumping, and climbing. Enabler.

Tier 2: Heavy Hitter. Your unarmed attacks deal 1 additional point of damage. Enabler.

Tier 3: Agility Training Pays Off. You are trained in Speed defense tasks. Enabler.

Tier 4: Grab and Toss (4 Might points). You attempt to grab a foe your size or smaller. If you succeed, you spin and toss your foe up to 20 feet (6 m) from you. Your foe lands prone and takes 5 points of damage from the impact (and possibly worse, depending on the landing site). Action.

Usurp Cypher, page 37

Excels Physically GM Intrusions: *An amazingly painful muscle cramp has to be stretched out. Fatigue sets in from too much working out earlier. Something lifted, broken, or thrown shatters unexpectedly.*

Excels Physically is a draggable focus.

Excels Physically Equipment:
Ardeyn: *Simple Ardeyn clothing, spare set of Ardeyn clothing, perspiration rag, a weapon of your choice, and 30 crowns.*
Ruk: *Ruk clothing, a sweet-sweat graft, an umbilical, a variable-weight module for exercise anywhere, a weapon of your choice, a knife, and 10 bits.*

Tier 5: Phenomenal Athlete. You add 2 points to your Speed Pool and 2 points to your Might Pool. Enabler.

Tier 6: Elite Athlete. You gain +1 to Armor and add 5 points to each of your three stat Pools. Enabler.

FIGHTS ALIENS

Aliens are by definition impossible to understand, except for the violent ones. Aliens that are all teeth and digestive enzymes are the easiest ones to deal with. It's the aliens with no clear motive that are the more subtle threat. Some aliens even pretend to be friendly. They give gifts. They offer hope. But you've seen it go bad all too often, and you'll not be fooled again.

You always carry weapons ideal for fighting aliens, and you don't hide that. You might even wear clothing or armor branded with the slogan "FIGHTS ALIENS" just so your intentions are plain.

Many alien fighters are vectors, but sometimes spinners choose this focus because they are good at ferreting out that which should not exist in the world.

Connection: If this is your starting focus, choose one of the following connections.

1. Pick one other PC. That character's sibling was duplicated and replaced by an alien (you're pretty sure).

2. Pick one other PC. You inaccurately identified that character as an alien, though you figured out your error before much harm could be done. The character may feel differently.

3. Pick one other PC. She knows a secret of yours: one of your parents is an alien.

4. Pick one other PC. That character saved you from an alien attack that would have ended in your death.

Equipment: Clothing appropriate to your recursion (in Ruk, a brightly colored bodysuit and an umbilical), alien sketchbook, two weapons of your choice, and an account with 100 bits.

> **Fights Aliens GM Intrusions:** *An NPC decides that you are clinically paranoid. You inaccurately determine an ally to be an alien fake. Your hand (or an ally's hand) is secretly replaced with an alien duplicate.*

```
● ○ ○ ▬▬▬▬▬▬▬
```

ALIEN

The word "alien" has different contexts depending on the recursion where this focus is offered, and the GM determines whether a creature fits the definition. In Ruk, the word means any nonhumanoid entity spawned from a prime world other than Earth or a recursion that hosts "alien" entities, though there is quite a bit of wiggle room in the middle. If a demon from Hell Frozen Over, a green one from Old Mars, or an AI from Cataclyst were to appear in Ruk, they would be considered aliens for the purposes of this focus. Strangers and creatures from the Qinod Singularity are also aliens.
```
▬▬▬▬▬▬▬ ○ ● ○
```

Minor Effect Suggestion: If your target is an alien, your attack (or its results) reveals its true nature to anyone else around.

Major Effect Suggestion: An alien of level 6 or less becomes intimidated by your single-minded fury and flees if you allow it. If you do not allow it, the alien loses its next turn trying to get away.

Tier 1: Spot the Alien (1+ Intellect point). A favorite alien trick is to replace a regular person with a nearly exact duplicate, one that might even believe she is the original, but whose real purpose is to infiltrate society and take it over from within. If you use this ability on a target within short range of level 2 or less, you can detect if that person has been replaced with a duplicate, fake, clone, or other facsimile. Instead of applying Effort to decrease the difficulty, you can apply Effort to increase the maximum level of the target. Thus, to identify a level 4 target (two levels above the normal limit), you must apply two levels of Effort. Action.

Alien Fighter. You inflict 2 additional points of damage when fighting creatures the GM identifies as alien. Enabler.

Tier 2: Alien Hunter. When tracking, looking for, interacting with, or hiding from aliens, the difficulty of the task is decreased by one step. Enabler.

Tier 3: Resist Alien Influence. You have gained a measure of resistance over alien mind control. You are trained in Intellect defense tasks. Enabler.

Tier 4: Improved Alien Fighter. You inflict 3 additional points of damage when fighting creatures the GM identifies as alien. Enabler.

Tier 5: Master Combatant. Choose one type of attack: light bashing, light bladed, light ranged, medium bashing, medium bladed, medium ranged, heavy bashing, heavy bladed, or heavy ranged. You are trained in attacks using that type of weapon. If you're already trained in that type of attack, you instead become specialized in that type of attack. Enabler.

Tier 6: Alien Death Spiral (3 Speed points). You can attack all foes within immediate range, whether they are aliens or not. Make separate attack rolls for each foe, but all attacks count as a single action in a single round. You remain limited by the amount of Effort you can apply on one action. Anything that modifies your attack or damage applies to all attacks. If you hit an alien with this attack, you inflict 1 additional point of damage. Action.

 ## FIRES A BLASTER

Nearly anyone who picks up a blaster, no matter how inexperienced, can really ruin someone else's day. But you're in a different class from "nearly anyone." You've made a study of blasters. It's possible that in your line of work, blaster practice is mandatory because to do otherwise would be to perish under the weapon fire of your many foes. On the other hand, you might just be a particularly violent hobbyist.

You wear clothing designed to avoid the notice of officials, though you don't hide your gun belt where you carry your blaster. Beneath your clothing, you also wear a slicksuit in case you need to slip away suddenly if things don't go your way.

The focus attracts many vectors, but spinners who want to back up their words with the business end of a blaster are also drawn to this focus.

Fires a Blaster GM Intrusions: *The blaster grows so hot that you must drop it for a few rounds or take damage. The blaster runs out of charge (or other exotic ammunition). Blaster fire ricochets in an unexpected direction.*

A blaster is a general term for any light, medium, or heavy ranged weapon (usually in the form of a gun or rifle) that emits lasers, high-energy particles, spikes, spores, flechettes, or some other advanced-technology ammunition. Most blasters can be used as rapid-fire weapons.

Connection: If this is your starting focus, choose one of the following connections.

1. Pick one other PC. That character is the one who asked you to deliver a parcel desired by ambushers who wanted it more than they cared about your life. Defending yourself (and the parcel) wakened your talent for aiming blasters.

2. Pick one other PC. That character once lent you a blaster that belonged to her relative, and it's the weapon that you still use.

3. Pick one other PC. You once killed someone while defending that character, though local authorities never found out the truth.

4. Pick one other PC. She treated you after you were nearly killed in a blaster fight outside a bar.

Equipment: Clothing appropriate to your recursion (in Ruk, a bodysuit and an umbilical), slicksuit, light armor, a blaster of your choice (light, medium, or heavy), and an account with 50 bits.

Tier 1: Practiced With Blasters. You are practiced with using blasters and suffer no penalty when using one. If you're already practiced with using blasters, you instead deal 1 additional point of damage with them. Enabler.

Tier 2: Shot on the Run (1 Speed point). You move up to a short distance and attack with your blaster without suffering any penalties. Action.

Blaster Maintenance. You are trained in all tasks related to repairing and recharging your personal blaster (and blasters that use a similar technology). Enabler.

Tier 3: Trained Blaster User. If you're not already trained in using blasters, you are now trained in using them. If you're already trained, you instead gain +1 to your Speed Edge. Enabler.

Tier 4: Blaster Trick. When you apply Effort to inflict more damage with a blaster, you inflict 4 additional points of damage (instead of 3). Enabler.

Tier 5: Specialized Blaster User. If you're not already specialized in using blasters, you are now specialized in using them. If you're already specialized, you instead gain +1 to your Speed Edge. Enabler.

Tier 6: Blaster Grenade (2+ Intellect points). You can take advantage of the fact that the weapon you use is charged with deadly energy or other exotic material. You fiddle with your blaster in just the right way to convert it into a grenadelike device that you throw at a target

Slicksuit, page 93

within short range. The blaster explosion inflicts 8 points of damage to all targets within immediate range. If you use Effort to increase the damage, each level applied inflicts 2 additional points (instead of 3), but creatures in the area take 1 point of damage even if missed by the attack. You can use this ability only once per blaster because the weapon is destroyed in the detonation.

Special Shot. When you hit a target with your blaster attack, you can choose to reduce the damage by 1 point but hit the target in a precise spot for a special effect. Possible effects include (but are not limited to):

• You can shoot an object out of someone's hand.

• You can shoot the leg, wing, or other limb it uses to move, limiting it to an immediate movement speed for a few days or until it receives expert medical care.

• You can shoot a strap holding a backpack, armor, or similarly strapped-on item so that it falls off. Enabler.

Goes Berserk GM Intrusions: *You go berserk when startled or angered. While berserk, you run through spikes, fire, or another damaging area and don't care. While berserk, you grab an ally and use him as an impromptu weapon.*

GOES BERSERK

Something hurt you. It smashed you, bruised you, tore at you, and pushed you well past all your previous limits. You almost didn't survive. Mercy, hope, and love dissolved in your torment. Rage saved you. You tapped a core of incandescent fury, kindled by the very treatment designed to break you. When the fury overtook you, it was a sweet madness that lifted you away from the world, where everything was white light and simple movements. When you went berserk, you made *everyone* pay.

The experience that made you into a berserker may have been instigated by you as part of a ritual to become a warrior beyond compare, or it could have been an unexpected and unwelcome event. Either way, now that you can tap the anger, you've learned to be especially careful with it, because when you go berserk, all your regular relationships fall away, and all that remains is kill.

Your hair is short, your clothing sparse, and your skin is probably elaborately scarified and tattooed in a fashion that marks you as a berserker.

Connection: If this is your starting focus, choose one of the following connections.

1. Pick one other PC. If that character is next to you and takes no action other than to remain next to you, you don't attack him when you go berserk.

2. Pick one other PC. You almost killed that character when you went berserk once, and you still feel bad about it, regardless of whether that character has forgiven you.

3. Pick one other PC. While that character is next to you, the difficulty of Intellect defense rolls to avoid going berserk is increased by one step.

4. Pick one other PC. While that character is next to you, the difficulty of Intellect defense rolls to avoid going berserk is reduced by one step.

Equipment: Ardeyn clothing (or equivalent), light armor, one weapon of your choice, a bone talisman, tools for creating new scarification designs, and 20 crowns.

Minor Effect Suggestion: You can end your rage immediately if you wish.

Major Effect Suggestion: You are in full control of your actions while you are berserk on your next turn.

GOING BERSERK

As a berserker, you're not in full control of yourself. When you take damage in combat (or inflict damage upon yourself), you might enter a state of insane rage, whether you wish to or not. Anytime you take damage in combat, you must make an Intellect defense roll whose difficulty is equal to the damage you take; if you fail, you go berserk. If you succeed, you don't go berserk, even if you want to (you can't choose not to make this defense roll, though you can choose not to apply Effort).

In addition, sometimes you spontaneously go berserk when angered, surprised, or scared. When this happens, the GM may allow you to attempt a difficulty 4 Intellect defense roll to avoid going berserk.

Once you are berserk, you remain so for up to ten minutes, unless you succeed on a difficulty 4 Intellect-based task to return to normal. When you return to your normal state of mind and body immediately after going berserk, the difficulty of all tasks you attempt is increased by one step for one hour, and you can't go berserk again until after your next ten-hour recovery roll.

"An hour after Emma translated into Ardeyn, she went fucking berserk! You have to respect that. Then run."
—Torah "The Windmill" Bishop

Tier 1: Berserk. When you go berserk (see the Going Berserk sidebar), you gain +8 to your Might Pool, +1 to your Might Edge, +2 to your Speed Pool, and +1 to your Speed Edge. While berserk, you attack every living creature within short range, starting with the closest. If no living creature is within short range, you move to seek out potential victims. Action to go berserk (whether you want to go berserk or not).

Tier 2: Unarmored Fighter. While unarmored, you are trained in Speed defense tasks (whether or not you are berserk). Enabler.

Tier 3: Shake It Off. When you return to your normal state of mind and body after going berserk, you do not suffer the increase in difficulty of tasks (see the Going Berserk sidebar). Enabler.

Tier 4: Controlled Berserking. Going berserk or returning to your normal state is now a difficulty 1 Intellect task. Enabler.

Tier 5: Enhanced Berserking. When you go berserk (see the Going Berserk sidebar), you gain +11 to your Might Pool, +1 to your Might Edge, +4 to your Speed Pool, +1 to your Speed Edge, and +2 to Armor. This replaces the benefits of the tier 1 power Berserk. Enabler.

Tier 6: Incarnation of Rage (4+ Intellect points). While berserk, you retain your rational mind for two rounds. You can apply Effort to extend this period of rationality. Thus, to remain rational for four rounds (two rounds longer than normal), you'd apply two levels of Effort. Enabler.

Supers recursion, page 27

Grows to Towering Heights GM Intrusions: *Rapid growth knocks over furnishings or smashes through ceilings or hanging lights. While enlarged, you break through the floor. People scream and run. An unexpected side effect from an energy attack causes you to shrink.*

GROWS TO TOWERING HEIGHTS

You have the ability to become a towering giant for short periods. When you do, everything and everyone seems to shrink around you, until it's like you're walking through a children's play area, where everything is sized for toddlers. As you grow ever larger, your sense of scale shifts further. At your maximum height, most other creatures are as insects, and unless you take care, you easily crush them beneath your colossal feet.

When you're not growing, you look normal. Only the clothing in direct contact with your skin grows with you, so you wear expensive outerwear only when you're fairly certain you won't have to trigger your Enlarge ability. If you choose this focus in a Supers recursion, you probably wear a colorful suit beneath your outerwear, allowing you to step "up" into your alter-ego at a moment's notice.

Vectors are most likely to choose this focus.

Connection: If this is your starting focus, choose one of the following connections.

1. Pick one other PC. When you grow, if that character is next to you, she also grows, but only about a foot in height.

2. Pick one other PC. That character helped you find a way to mentally control your ability to grow; at first, it triggered only when you were emotionally distressed.

3. Pick two other PCs. At great risk to themselves, they pulled your oversized, unconscious body from a bad situation and saved your life.

4. Pick one other PC. This character inadvertently hinders your actions. If he is within immediate range, the difficulty of any action that you take related to this focus is increased by one step.

Equipment: Clothing appropriate to your recursion (in Ruk, a bodysuit and an umbilical; in a Supers recursion, a suit and a utility belt) and an account with 50 bits.

Minor Effect Suggestion: Your opponent is so startled by your size that it is dazed, during which time the difficulty of all tasks it performs is modified by one step to its detriment.

Major Effect Suggestion: All opponents within short range are so startled by your sudden growth that they are dazed, during which time the difficulty of all tasks they perform is modified by one step to their detriment.

Tier 1: Enlarge (1+ Might point). You trigger the enzymatic reaction that draws additional mass from a quantum recursion, and you (and your clothing or suit) grow larger. You achieve a height of 9 feet (3 m) and stay that way for about a minute. During that time, you add 4 points to your Might Pool, add +1 to Armor, and add +2 to your Might Edge. While you are larger than normal, the difficulty of your Speed defense rolls is increased by one step, and you are practiced in using your fists as heavy weapons.

When the effects of Enlarge end, your Armor and Might Edge return to normal, and you subtract a number of points from your Might Pool equal to the number you gained (if this brings the pool to 0, subtract the overflow first from your Speed Pool and then, if necessary, from your Intellect Pool). Each additional time you use Enlarge before your next ten-hour recovery roll, you must apply an additional level of Effort. Thus, the second time you use Enlarge, you must apply one level of Effort; the third time you use Enlarge, two levels of Effort; and so on.

Action to initiate.

Freakishly Large. Your increased size intimidates most people. While you enjoy the effects of Enlarge, the difficulty of all intimidation tasks you attempt is decreased by one step. Enabler.

Tier 2: Bigger. When you use Enlarge, you can choose to grow up to 12 feet (4 m) in height, and you add a total of 7 temporary points to your Might Pool. Enabler.

Advantages of Being Big. You're so big that you can move massive objects more easily, climb buildings by using hand- and footholds unavailable to regular-sized people, and jump much farther. While you enjoy the effects of Enlarge, the difficulty of all climbing, lifting, and jumping tasks is decreased by one step. Enabler.

Tier 3: Huge. When you use Enlarge, you can choose to grow up to 16 feet (5 m) in height. When you do, you add +1 to Armor (a total of +2 to Armor) and deal 2 additional points of damage with melee attacks. Enabler.

Tier 4: Grab. While you are Enlarged, you can attack by attempting to wrap your massive hands around a target the size of a normal human or smaller. While you maintain your hold as your action, you keep the target from moving or taking physical actions (other than attempts to escape). The target's escape attempt is modified by two steps to its detriment due to your size. If you wish, you can automatically inflict 3 points of damage each round on the target while you hold it, but you can also keep it protected (by taking all attacks otherwise meant for the target). Action.

Tier 5: Gargantuan. When you use Enlarge, you can choose to grow up to 30 feet (9 m) in height, and you add a total of 10 temporary points to your Might Pool. Enabler.

Tier 6: Colossal. When you use Enlarge, you can choose to grow up to a base height of 60 feet (18 m). When you do, you add a total of 15 temporary points to your Might Pool, and you deal a total of 4 additional points of damage with melee attacks. For each level of Effort you apply to increase your height further, your total height increases by 10 feet (3 m), and you add 1 point to your Might Pool. Thus, the first time you use Enlarge after a ten-hour recovery roll, if you apply two levels of Effort, your base height is 80 feet (24 m), and you add a total of 17 temporary points to your Might Pool. Enabler.

In Ruk, a special genetic makeup paired with a growth-hormone-accelerating graft makes the Grows to Towering Heights focus possible.

> ● ○ ○ ▬▬▬▬▬▬
>
> ## GROWING TO TOWERING HEIGHTS
> Once a character becomes so large that she towers over buildings, she can accomplish a variety of tasks that a GM can adjudicate. For instance, a character who is 120 feet (37 m) tall covers a short distance (up to 50 feet [15 m]) with her average stride, and if she spent her action moving, she'd cover about 500 feet (152 m) instead. She could attempt to use her Grab ability on targets much larger than a regular-sized human, make melee attacks against airplanes, leave behind enormous footprints that might serve as pits, and so on.
>
> ▬▬▬▬▬▬▬▬▬ ● ○ ○

HUNTS ZOMBIES

Those fucking things have to die. They killed your mom, your dad, your brother. They killed your partner. Zombies killed your *dog*. The time for cowering behind barricades is over. You've got nothing left to live for, except kill zed. Maybe you tell yourself you do it to safeguard future generations or to ensure that the American way of life isn't snuffed. Some days, it's even true. But really, you do it for revenge. Each time an HRV-positive shambler's head explodes, you smile.

You typically wear biker's leathers, helmet, and gloves, and you strap on a utility belt to carry your ammo and other needful things.

Eradicating zombies is something anyone can get behind or be motivated by circumstance to undertake. That said, those who choose Hunts Zombies as a focus are usually vectors.

Connection: If this is your starting focus, choose one of the following connections.

1. Pick one other PC. If that character is next to you and is attacked by a zombie, you can choose to take the attack instead.

2. Pick one other PC. You worry that character might be carrying an unhealthy HRV viral load, and you keep a close eye on her in case she converts.

3. Pick one other PC. He once saved you from a zombie. You're not quite sure how to handle that.

4. Pick one other PC. The character strongly reminds you of one of your family members or friends who was killed by zed.

Equipment: Clothing, riding leathers (light armor), motorcycle helmet, leather gloves, two weapons of your choice, a lethal dose of morphine for yourself "just in case," and $300.

Minor Effect Suggestion: You disable (or completely remove) the zombie's arm, which keeps it busy for one round as it figures out how to attack with its other arm and mouth.

Major Effect Suggestion: The zombie's head nearly comes off, which confuses it for a round as its head lolls. In subsequent rounds, the difficulty of the zombie's attacks and defenses is modified by one step to its detriment.

Tier 1: Tracker and Hunter. When tracking, looking for, interacting with, or hiding from zombies, the difficulty of the task is decreased by one step. Enabler.

Zombie Fighter. You inflict 3 additional points of damage when fighting zombies. Enabler.

Tier 2: Defense Against Zombies. Zombies bite, spit, claw, or use more frightening forms of attack. You are trained in one type of defense of your choice. Enabler.

Tier 3: Stay Down. Normally, if an attack would reduce a zombie's health to 0, it does so only if the number rolled in the attack was even; otherwise, the zombie is reduced to 1 point of health instead. But the Stay Down ability lets you ignore this rule. It doesn't matter if your attack roll is even or odd—only whether you hit the zombie. Stay Down also disables the healing abilities that some zombies possess. Enabler.

Stawicki '14

Expert Combatant. Choose one type of attack in which you are not already trained: light bashing, light bladed, light ranged, medium bashing, medium bladed, medium ranged, heavy bashing, heavy bladed, or heavy ranged. You are trained in attacks using that type of weapon. Enabler.

Tier 4: Horde Fighting. When two or more foes attack you at once in melee, you can use them against each other. The difficulty of your attack rolls against them is reduced by one step. Enabler.

Tier 5: Zombie Defender. The difficulty of all your defense rolls to avoid zombie attacks is decreased by one step. Enabler.

Tier 6: Master Combatant. Choose one type of attack: light bashing, light bladed, light ranged, medium bashing, medium bladed, medium ranged, heavy bashing, heavy bladed, or heavy ranged. You are trained in attacks using that type of weapon. If you're already trained in that type of attack, you instead become specialized in that type of attack. Enabler.

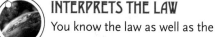

INTERPRETS THE LAW

You know the law as well as the back of your hand. Broad mandates, narrow rulings, well-meaning overreaches, regulatory considerations, and outright loopholes in the law are all the tools you need to twist outcomes to suit your desire. Knowledge is power, which is why many people who have crossed you now fear you. It's your decision whether you put your prowess toward noble causes or use it for your own aggrandizement.

You wear nice suits and designer sunglasses, carry a briefcase, and walk around in shoes that cost more than many people earn in a month.

Spinners and Interprets the Law go together like congressional delegates and unregulated PAC spending.

Connection: If this is your starting focus, choose one of the following connections.

Interprets the Law GM Intrusions: *The law has changed since you last researched it. You have a coughing fit during an important speech. You left a briefcase of files in the car.*

1. Pick one other PC. That character seriously hurt someone in an altercation, but you got her off with no charges. She may feel grateful or ashamed.

2. Pick one other PC. He borrowed your copy of *The Prince* by Niccolò Machiavelli and still hasn't returned it.

3. Pick one other PC. You once defended him in a court of law but suffered one of your very few defeats because of the case or perhaps your own failing—you're not sure which.

4. Pick one other PC. That character has confided in you that she hates "bloodsucking lawyers" and is glad you're not one. You haven't decided yet if you're going to reveal your profession to her.

Equipment: Suit, sunglasses, briefcase, extra pens, light handgun, leather wallet or purse, nice shoes, and $500.

Minor Effect Suggestion: The target is confused, causing it to stumble and drop whatever it's holding.

Major Effect Suggestion: The target can't believe what you just said and is dazed and unable to take actions for a round as it tries to reconcile your statement with reality.

Tier 1: Opening Statement. You're trained in tasks related to persuasion, deception, and detecting the falsehoods of others. Enabler.

Knowledge of the Law. You're trained in the law of the land. If you don't know the answer to a question of law, you know where and how to research it (a university's law library is a good place to start, but you've also got online sources). Enabler.

Tier 2: Debate (3 Intellect points). In any gathering of two or more people trying to establish the truth or come to a decision, you can sway the verdict with masterful rhetoric. If you are given one minute or more to argue your point, either the decision goes your way or, if someone else effectively argues a competing point, the difficulty of any associated persuasion or deception task is decreased by two steps. One minute to initiate.

Tier 3: Able Assistance. When you help someone with a task related to research or codified knowledge, you always reduce the difficulty of the task by one step regardless of your own skill at that task. Enabler.

Keen Mind. You gain +1 to your Intellect Edge.

Tier 4: Objection (3 Intellect points). Your vociferous, booming objection to a target's intended action prevents it from taking any action (including attacking or defending itself from an attack) for one round. Each additional time you attempt this ability against the same target, you must apply one additional level of Effort than you applied on the previous attempt. Action.

Tier 5: No One Knows Better. You are trained in two of the following skills: persuasion, deception, intimidation, research, knowledge in one area, or seeing through deception. If you choose a skill in which you're already trained, you become specialized in that skill instead. Enabler.

Tier 6: Master Barrister. You add 5 points to your Intellect Pool.

Legal Intern. You gain a level 4 follower who is mostly interested in helping with your law-related tasks, but who might also help you in other areas. Enabler.

 ## IS A CYBORG

You have been rebuilt with advanced biomechanical technology, infusing your nerves with optical filaments that propagate signals much faster than normal flesh could ever hope to match. Once you get the kinks worked out, one of your arms has the ability to metamorphose into an energy weapon when you will it. You're more resistant to harm than before and much faster. If one word could be used to describe you, it would be "better."

Though you're a cyborg, you retain your previous shape and size from before you were rebuilt. That said, if someone were to take a close look at you, they'd notice tiny silvery filaments running beneath your skin, pulsing with dim radiance. When your energy weapon is deployed, it's much more obvious that you're partially artificial.

Paradoxes and vectors are equally drawn to this focus. Paradoxes enjoy the increased access to data (with extra protection thrown in), while vectors excel with the heightened reaction potential.

Connection: If this is your starting focus, choose one of the following connections.

1. Pick one other PC. That character is partially responsible for an accident you suffered that required you to become a cyborg to save your life.

2. Pick one other PC. That character seems very leery of your cybernetic parts (although this might just be your perception).

3. Pick one other PC. She knows a secret command word that triggers a hidden AI built into your nerve system. When triggered, the AI commandeers your body for one minute. The difficulty of all actions taken by the AI is modified by one step in its favor, but its motivations are suspect.

4. Pick one other PC. That character was one of the technicians who helped to rebuild you.

Equipment: Clothing appropriate to your recursion (in Ruk, a bodysuit and an umbilical), a weapon of your choice, a multimeter, and an account with 50 bits.

Minor Effect Suggestion: Your integrated cyborg circuitry learns from your successful actions. You gain a +1 bonus to rolls involving a similar task (such as making attacks against the same foe or operating the same device).

Major Effect Suggestion: You can take an immediate extra action.

Legal intern: level 4; health 12; inflicts 4 points of damage

Is a Cyborg GM Intrusions: *A short circuit causes you to wrongly classify an ally as a foe. A reboot freezes you for a couple of rounds. An accidental electrical discharge fries a piece of useful equipment. Someone shows up with a remote control to your systems.*

Tier 1: Traded Flesh for Synthetic. Portions of your skin and bone have been replaced with tougher, synthetic material that grants you +1 to Armor and +1 to your Speed Edge. Enabler.

Machine Affinity. You are trained in all tasks involving machines. Enabler.

Tier 2: Forearm Energy Weapon. You can spend an action to metamorphose your machinelike hand and forearm into the weapon that replaced your original limb. You are practiced with this medium weapon, which fires beam energy at a target within short range. Each time you engage your weapon, you can use it for about a minute (or until you roll a natural 1 on an attack) before it needs to recharge for another minute. Action to initiate; action to regain normal use of arm.

Tier 3: Electric Reactions. You add 5 points to your Speed Pool. Enabler.

Tier 4: Overclock (5 Speed points). You take an extra action. You can't use this ability more than once per turn (but see Uberclock, below). Enabler.

Tier 5: Recharge. You can hold a cypher or certain artifacts with compatible power systems and drain them of their charge as an action. You gain a number of points equal to the level of the device drained, and you immediately add them to any of your stat Pools. Any additional points beyond your Pools' maximums are lost. Action.

Tier 6: Uberclock. When you use Overclock, you can apply Effort to increase the number of extra actions you can take. For each two levels of Effort applied, you can take one additional extra action. Thus, to take three extra actions (two more than normally allowed), you must apply four levels of Effort. Enabler.

Is Idolized by Millions
GM Intrusions: Fans are endangered or hurt on your behalf. Someone in your entourage betrays you. Your show, tour, contract, or other event is canceled. The media posts photos of you in an embarrassing situation.

IS IDOLIZED BY MILLIONS

Some celebrities are known for their talent, while others are simply known for being known. However the spotlight found you, you're a celebrity now, and people love you—often a little too much. You can't go anywhere publicly without people recognizing you, approaching you for a shared selfie, or pointing at you from afar. Whenever you do anything, whether it's going to the beach, adopting a new pet, or going out clubbing, the event becomes pablum for celebrity TV shows and websites, which often twist the facts into a caricature of reality. But hey, like your publicists say, no PR is bad PR.

You wear oversized sunglasses, designer clothing, and expensive shoes that are also comfortable.

Spinners and vectors are equally likely to be celebrities.

Connection: If this is your starting focus, choose one of the following connections.

1. Pick one other PC. You were childhood friends. As you got famous, she continued to live a normal life, and you worry that she resents you.

2. Pick one other PC. That character knows that though you're quick with a smile, as if having the time of your life, on the inside you feel empty and alone.

3. Pick one other PC. That character once called you a "narcissistic douchecopter" on social media. You're not sure if it was a joke.

4. Pick one other PC. The media thinks that you and that character have a secret relationship and uses any pretext to revisit the story and give it new life.

Equipment: Designer sunglasses and clothing, Versace purse or wallet, a smartphone, a few pens for signing autographs, business cards with your website, and $500.

Minor Effect Suggestion: Your foe realizes who you are and leaves himself open; the difficulty of your next attack is reduced by one step.

Major Effect Suggestion: Nearby strangers recognize you, scream your name, and run to get your autograph, shielding you from enemy attacks for a couple of rounds.

Tier 1: Entourage. Your entourage (five level 1 twenty-somethings) accompanies you wherever you go unless you purposefully disband it for a particular outing. You can ask them to deliver things for you, run messages, pick up your dry cleaning—pretty much whatever you want, within reason. They can also run interference if you're trying to avoid someone, help hide you from media attention, help you muscle through a crowd, and so on. On the other hand, if a situation becomes physically violent, they retreat to safety. Enabler.

Talent. You are trained in one of the following areas: writing, journalism, a particular style of art, a particular sport, chess, science communication, acting, news presentation, or some related area that led to your celebrity. Enabler.

Tier 2: Perks of Stardom. You are adept at claiming the rewards that fame can generate. When you are recognized, you can be seated at any restaurant, be let into any government building, be invited to any show or sports event (even if they're sold out), get a seat at a private function of any sort, or get into any club, no matter how exclusive. When dealing with

someone who can't or won't immediately give in to your desire, you gain an asset on all tasks related to persuasion if that person recognizes you or is convinced that you're a celebrity even if he doesn't recognize you. Enabler.

Tier 3: Devoted Groupie. You gain a level 3 groupie who is completely devoted to you and follows you wherever you go (probably someone in your entourage makes this transition). You and the GM must work out the details. You'll probably make rolls for your groupie when he takes actions. A groupie in combat usually doesn't make separate attacks but instead helps you with yours. On your action, if the groupie is next to you, he serves as an asset for one attack you make on your turn. If you lose your groupie for any reason, you gain a new one after at least two weeks pass. Enabler.

Tier 4: Captivate With Starshine. For as long as you speak, you keep the attention of all level 2 NPCs who can hear you. If you also have the Enthrall twist, you can similarly captivate all level 3 NPCs. Action to initiate.

Capable Groupie. Your groupie increases to level 4. Enabler.

Tier 5: Do You Know Who I Am (3 Intellect points)? Acting only as someone who is famous and used to privilege can, you verbally harangue a living foe who can hear you so forcefully that it is unable to take any action, including making attacks, for one round. Whether you succeed or fail, the difficulty of the next action the target takes after your attempt is modified by one step to its detriment. Action.

Tier 6: Transcend the Script (5 Intellect points). Whether they were lines you wrote, acted, reported on, or otherwise incorporated into your talent, you compose an oratory on the fly that is so wonderful that even you believe it. For each ally who hears it (and you, too), the difficulty of a task attempted within the next hour is decreased by two steps.

Zealous Groupie. Your groupie increases to level 5. Enabler.

Devoted groupie: *level 3; health 9; inflicts 3 points of damage*

Enthrall, page 39

Capable groupie: *level 4; health 12; inflicts 4 points of damage*

Zealous groupie: *level 5; health 15; inflicts 5 points of damage*

Keeps a Magic Ally GM
Intrusions: *The creature*
unexpectedly disappears
into its bound object. The
bound object cracks. The
creature disagrees with you
and doesn't do as asked.
The creature tells you that
it's leaving unless you agree
to perform some task for it.

Magic creature: *level 3;*
health 9

KEEPS A MAGIC ALLY

You discovered, were given, or otherwise obtained an allied magic creature bound to an object (perhaps a djinni in a lamp, but work with your GM if either of you would prefer a different kind of creature and object). It requires a fair bit of your attention and energy to keep the djinni happy and satisfied, but it's usually worth the effort. The djinni grants you aid and companionship, and eventually it may grant minor wishes.

You wear comfortable, flashy, and somewhat striking clothing, possibly provided by your magic ally, who is at pains to tell you how fabulous you look, even if others suggest that you've gone overboard.

Connection: If this is your starting focus, choose one of the following connections.

1. Pick one other PC. She gave you the lamp

as a present. Only afterward did it become apparent that a magic creature lived inside.

2. Pick one other PC. You promised that character that one day you'd ask the djinni to grant you a wish to bring back her dead sibling, parent, or friend. However, you're not sure that your ally can accomplish that wish or what the result will look like.

3. Pick one other PC. He returned the lamp to you after thieves stole it. It's possible that he wants a reward.

4. Pick one other PC. That character is half convinced that your djinni is a servant of evil, perhaps a demon in disguise, and he is watching you for signs of demonic influence.

Equipment: A lamp or other object, clothing somewhat more striking than is common for your recursion (in Ardeyn, a feathered headdress, layers of brightly colored silks, semiprecious jewelry, and a silver cape), light armor, a weapon of your choice, an explorer's pack, and 100 crowns.

Minor Effect Suggestion: The difficulty of the next task attempted by your magic ally is decreased by one step.

Major Effect Suggestion: Your magic ally can take an immediate extra action of its choice (possibly making an attack on its own).

Tier 1: Bound Magic Creature. You possess a magic creature bound to a physical object (perhaps a djinni bound to a lamp, a demon bound to a coin, or a spirit bound to a mirror). The magic creature doesn't (yet) have the full power that one of its kind could possess when mature. Normally, the creature remains quiescent in its bound object. When you spend an action to manifest it, it appears next to you as a level 3 creature (if a djinni, as a humanoid of somewhat exotic appearance and dress) that can converse with you. The creature has its own personality determined by the GM and is a level higher than its base level for one area of knowledge (such as local history). The creature may have a long-term goal of its own, if the GM determines.

Each time the creature becomes physically manifest, it remains so for up to one hour. During that period, it accompanies you and follows your instructions. The creature must remain an immediate distance from you; if it moves farther away, it is yanked back into its object at the end of your following turn and cannot return until after your next ten-hour recovery roll. It doesn't attack creatures, but it can spend its action to serve as an asset for any one attack you make on your turn. Otherwise, it can take actions on its own (though you'll likely roll for it).

If the creature is reduced to 0 health, it dissipates. It reforms in its object in 1d6 + 2 days.

If you lose the bound object, you retain a sense of the direction in which it lies.

Action to manifest magic creature.

Tier 2: Object Bond (3 Intellect points). When you manifest your allied creature, it can move up to 300 feet (91 m) from you before being returned to its bound object. In addition, it can remain manifest for an extended period, lasting until the end of your next ten-hour recovery roll. Finally, if you give permission, the creature can emerge from and enter the bound object on its own initiative. Enabler.

Hidden Closet. The allied creature can store items for you within its bound object, including extra sets of clothing, tools, food, and so on. The interior of the object is, in effect, a pocket dimension recursion that normally only the creature can access. The additional storage is equivalent to that of a large closet, and the creature can ferry only items that it can carry. Enabler.

Tier 3: Minor Wish. At your request, the allied creature can spend its action casting a minor spell on you. Afterward, it must retreat to its bound object to rest for at least one hour. The effects it can produce include the following. Action to initiate.

Golden Ward: You gain +1 to Armor for one hour from a translucent sheen of golden light.

Touch of Grace: With the allied creature's touch, you add 3 points to any stat Pool. If you are not damaged, you add the points to your chosen Pool's maximum. They remain until you expend them, you lose them to damage, or an hour passes.

Golden Anger: A golden light touches your eyes. For the next several minutes, if you attack a target, you inflict 2 additional points of damage.

Light of Truth: Whenever you attempt to discern falsehood during the next hour, the difficulty of the task is decreased by two steps.

Tier 4: Improved Object Bond (5 Intellect points). When you manifest your magic ally, it is a level 4 creature.

In addition, the creature gains a pulse attack that renders all artifacts, machines, and lesser magic devices within short range inoperable for one minute. After the creature uses this ability, it must retreat to its object to rest for a few hours. Enabler.

Tier 5: Moderate Wish. At your request, the allied creature can spend its action casting a moderate spell on you. Afterward, it must retreat to its bound object to rest for at least one hour. The effects it can produce include the following. Action to initiate.

Golden Armor: You gain +3 to Armor for one hour from a translucent sheen of golden light.

Improved Touch of Grace: With the allied creature's touch, you add 6 points to any stat Pool. If you are not damaged, you add the points to your chosen Pool's maximum. They remain until you expend them, you lose them to damage, or an hour passes.

Golden Fury: A golden light blazes in your eyes. For the next several minutes, if you attack a target, you inflict 5 additional points of damage.

Invisible: With a touch, the allied creature bends light that falls on you so you seem to disappear. You are invisible to other creatures for ten minutes. While invisible, you are specialized in stealth and Speed defense tasks. This effect ends if you do something to reveal your presence or position—attacking, using an ability, moving a large object, and so on. If this occurs, you can regain the remaining invisibility effect by taking an action to focus on hiding your position.

Tier 6: Object Bond Mastery (7 Intellect points). When you manifest your magic ally, it is a level 7 creature. It can remain manifest for only a few minutes, after which it must return to its object and rest for several days before you can manifest it again.

The creature can make its own magic touch

Improved magic creature: *level 4; health 12*

Masterful magic creature: *level 7; health 35; magic touch attack inflicts 9 points of damage; can transform into smoke and flame* attacks (when it does, you roll for it). If it uses its pulse attack from Improved Object Bond (tier 4), instead of deactivating items, the creature can take control of one item within short range for one minute, if applicable.

Finally, the creature can transform into smoke and flame as its action, giving it +10 to Armor but rendering it incapable of attacking foes. In this form, it can fly a long distance each round, and the first time each day it returns to flesh (as an action), it regains 25 points of health. Enabler.

LEARNS QUICKLY
You might not have the job of your dreams, but you do all right. Perhaps events beyond your control set you down a path that led to where you are today, making the best of a mediocre or even a bad situation. Or maybe you're young, and your break just hasn't come along yet; you're confident that it's right around the corner, maybe once you finish school. Either way, you work hard to get ahead, deal with bad situations as they arise, and learn quickly whether you're working retail, serving fast food, or loading trucks in the back of a warehouse.

You don't stand out in a crowd because you've learned that doing so can draw unwanted attention. That's why you usually wear nondescript clothing, cover up any ink you have, and wear glasses whether you need eye correction or not.

Spinners are most often drawn to this focus.

Connection: If this is your starting focus, choose one of the following connections.

1. Pick one other PC. That character helped you get your current job.

2. Pick one other PC. Through no fault of his own, that character got you fired from your last job by pointing out a problem with something you were connected to only indirectly.

3. Pick one other PC. That character is your cousin.

4. Pick one other PC. You're pretty sure that character hates your guts, though you don't know why.

Equipment: Modern clothing, a feature phone, two tickets to see a show at a local movie theater, and $100.

Minor Effect Suggestion: The difficulty of your next task, attack, or defense (if made within one minute) is decreased by one step.

Major Effect Suggestion: Treat the result of your next task, attack, or defense (if made within one minute) as if you rolled a natural 18.

Tier 1: Still Waters Run Deep. You have a greater-than-average capacity to think things through. You add 3 points to your Intellect Pool. Enabler.

There's Your Problem. You are trained in tasks related to figuring out how to solve problems with multiple solutions (like the best way to pack a truck, calm an enraged customer, give a cat a shot of insulin, or find a route through the city for maximum speed). Enabler.

Tier 2: Quick Study. You learn from repetitive actions. You gain a +1 bonus to rolls for similar tasks after the first time (such as operating the same device or making attacks against the same foe). Once you move on to a new task, the familiarity with the old task fades—unless you start doing it again.

Tier 3: Put It Behind You. You know that mentally dwelling on bad outcomes rarely

---

Learns Quickly was conceived as a focus for players who don't want to start the game with overt advantages, even social ones. On the other hand, it's a great focus for any character who relies on Intellect; many a tenured professor, researcher, or similarly skilled professional would find Learns Quickly a fabulous choice.

Learns Quickly Equipment:
Ardeyn: *Simple Ardeyn clothing, parchment, ink and quill, a weapon of your choice, a fish knife, and 10 crowns.*
Ruk: *Ruk clothing, an umbilical, a voice-memo graft, a weapon of your choice, a knife, and 10 bits.*

Learns Quickly GM Intrusions: *You are fired. An NPC recipient of criticism turns violent. You absent-mindedly lose your keys, a card, or another small but needful item.*

Learns Quickly is a draggable focus.

serves to improve matters. Moving on to whatever's next is the best way to cope. You gain +1 to your Intellect Edge. Enabler.

Hard to Distract. You are trained in Intellect defense tasks. Enabler.

Tier 4: Pay It Forward (3 Intellect points). You can pass on what you've learned. When you give another character a suggestion involving her next action that is not an attack, the difficulty of her action is decreased by one step for one minute. Action.

Tier 5: Phenomenal Learner. You add 3 points to your Intellect Pool.

I Know That. You are trained in one area of knowledge of your choice.

Tier 6: Two Things at Once (6 Intellect points). The ultimate test: you divide your attention and take two separate actions this round. Enabler.

MANIPULATES STRANGE ENERGY (SPECIAL FOCUS)

This focus becomes available only after you've translated at least one time. After that, you can choose this focus in whichever recursion you translate to.

You've made the Chaosphere a special study, and in doing so, you've become more adept at manipulating the dark energy of the Strange. Your emphasis on the Strange grants abilities that are useful both while you're within the Chaosphere and while you travel in other recursions with this focus active.

Paradoxes have the proper mindset for concentrating on the manipulation of the Strange, though sometimes spinners, especially those who enjoy helping others, find this focus appealing.

As someone who manipulates Strange energy, you probably wear at least one prominent tattoo of the iconic fractal "S" that designates the Strange.

Connection: This focus can't normally be your starting focus.

Equipment: Clothing appropriate to your starting recursion, light or medium armor, one weapon of your choice, a few grains of brachistochrone dust in a glass vial as a souvenir, and $200.

Minor Effect Suggestion: Even though you've used your cypher once, it still retains some power and can be used again.

Major Effect Suggestion: You step directly between the Strange and a recursion (you can't step from the Strange to Earth or from Earth to the Strange).

Tier 1: Cypher Adept. You can bear one additional cypher. Enabler.

Strange Knowledge. You are trained in tasks related to recalling information about the dark energy network of the Strange, which includes one or two well-known beacons (including the Orb of Worlds), one or two locations where you can move directly from a recursion into the Strange (including Port Jayeed in the recursion of Ardeyn), the danger of alienation, and other general knowledge about the Chaosphere. This training counts as a buffer of −1 against the effects of alienation. Enabler.

Orb of Worlds, page 221

Port Jayeed, page 174

Alienation, page 216

Inkling, page 273

Manipulates Strange Energy GM Intrusions: *Inklings always seem to find you. When alienation finally affects you, it hits twice as hard. Fundament created collapses unexpectedly or has dangerous resonance. Creatures of the Strange track you down for vengeance.*

Manipulates Strange Energy is a draggable focus.

Brachistochrone dust, page 219

When you adopt a new focus after Manipulates Strange Energy and have as many cyphers as your cypher limit allows, choose which one of them evaporates (as a result of losing the additional cypher granted by the Cypher Adept ability).

Chaosphere navigation, page 215

Fractal surfing, page 215

Fundament, page 214

Discerning Mind, page 13

Tier 2: Imbue Artifact (2+ Intellect points). You imbue an artifact with Strange energies, granting it the ability to translate in a fashion similar to a cypher. This is a difficulty 2 task. The artifact must be level 3 or lower. Instead of applying Effort to decrease the difficulty, you can apply Effort to increase the maximum level of the artifact you can imbue. Thus, to imbue a level 6 artifact (three levels above the normal limit), you must apply three levels of Effort. Action.

Chaosphere Navigation Training. You are trained in Chaosphere navigation. This training counts as a buffer of –1 against the effects of alienation. Enabler.

Tier 3: Intellect Fortress. You have +3 to Armor against damaging attacks and damaging effects that target the mind and Intellect. The difficulty of defense rolls against attacks that attempt to confuse, persuade, frighten, or otherwise influence you is decreased by one step. (If you also have the Discerning Mind spinner twist, you have +6 to Armor against these attacks and

effects, and the difficulty of defense against mental influence is decreased by two steps.) Enabler.

Fractal Surfing Training. You are trained in fractal surfing. This training counts as a buffer of –1 against the effects of alienation. Enabler.

Tier 4: Precipitate Fundament (5+ Intellect points). You can influence and manifest solid fractal shapes in the Strange known as fundament. While you are in the Strange, you can precipitate solid fundament to create an object within long range that could fit within a 10-foot (3 m) cube. This is a difficulty 2 Intellect-based task. The object of fundament is crude and can have no moving parts, but you could create a chamber or other structure to grant travelers a rest from the dark energy network. You could also create a portion of a larger structure, a rough sculpture, a crude craft to use for fractal surfing (the craft allows up to ten creatures to rely on a single creature's use of fractal surfing), and so on. The object of

fundament persists for as long as you remain within long range of it. If you apply two levels of Effort to increase the duration of the object, the object you create is permanent unless destroyed normally. Action.

Tier 5: Call Strange Creature (5 Intellect points). You send out a pulse of energy into the dark energy network, and a creature of the Strange is drawn to you a few rounds later. This is a difficulty 2 Intellect-based task. The GM determines the creature called, which could be a cypher eater, a dark energy pharaoh, an NPC recursor, or something else entirely. The creature you call isn't immediately hostile or bound to serve you. However, if you can communicate with it, the creature may be open to negotiation. It might also be hungry. Action to initiate.

Tier 6: Traveler of the Strange (6 Intellect points). When using a craft you created with Precipitate Fundament, you greatly decrease travel times within the Chaosphere. When you attempt to halve the travel time through the Strange to a known site, the difficulty of the task isn't increased by one step, nor do you get lost if you fail the attempt (as normally happens).

Furthermore, you can attempt to decrease the travel time to a known site dramatically. When you do, the difficulty of the task is increased to 5, and you do become lost if you fail. However, on a success, you reduce noted travel times from hours to minutes, from days to hours, from months to days, and from years to months. For instance, traveling to the House of Gears would normally take 3d6 + 12 months. If you succeed, the trip takes 3d6 + 12 days. Enabler.

MASTERS WUXIA

Others may believe you've learned everything about martial arts. They don't understand that yours is the student's path. Wuxia is your teacher, and you've pledged to study it for as long as you live. Each day is another attempt to strive for perfection, though you fully realize the journey is the important part. Whether you were trained in a secret dojo, drank a concoction crafted by an ancient sorcerer, or woke ancestral power in your blood, you are a wuxia hero, and you fight for what you believe is right.

You wear clothing that's both stylish and flexible enough to fight in, sometimes donning

House of Gears, page 226

Cypher eater, page 263

Dark energy pharaoh, page 264

Masters Wuxia GM Intrusions: *Three level 3 assassins who have been tracking you appear on the nearby rooftops. Doubt, disruption, or failure causes your elemental connection to falter until you succeed on a difficulty 3 Intellect-based task. Your elemental manifestation threatens, burns, or disrupts an ally.*

"Iron Flower Zi is my defeated foe."
—Bastard Wu

a sturdy leather coat to provide a bit of extra protection against the rigors of physical combat.

Wuxia heroes are most likely to be vectors.

Connection: If this is your starting focus, choose one of the following connections.

1. Pick one other PC. That character asked for help in defeating a bully, and you obliged.

2. Pick one other PC. You think you saw that character accept a package marked with a symbol of a secret society you have reason to distrust. You have yet to confront her about what you think you saw.

3. Pick one other PC. You call that character "Hawk" as a nickname. It's up to him whether the name is acceptable, but if it's not, sometimes you forget and use it anyway.

4. Pick one other PC. The character expressed interest in your heirloom ring or amulet, so you lent it out. She lost it.

Equipment: Modern clothing, leather trench coat (counts as light armor), hat, two weapons of your choice, an heirloom amulet or ring with an ancient symbol (unless your friend lost it), and $200.

Minor Effect Suggestion: The target's weapon is knocked from its hand. Retrieving it or drawing a new one means the next attack the target performs with the weapon is modified by one step to its detriment.

Major Effect Suggestion: Make an additional attack with your weapon on your turn.

Tier 1: Elemental Fist. Choose your preferred element: chi, fire, lightning, or shadow. When you attack with a melee weapon, which could be your unarmed attack, it is sheathed with a manifestation of your chosen element, which has the following effect.

Chi. Chi is not usually visible (unless you wish it). It is the distillation of your spirit rising to the surface of your mind and body. You move with additional grace and skill, adding 3 points to your Speed Pool. Enabler.

Fire. When you strike a target, it burns for 1 additional point of damage each round following your initial attack, unless it spends an action putting out the flames. Multiple strikes by you could cause multiple ignition points, but a target can put out all the flames by spending one action. Enabler.

Lightning. Either you inflict 1 additional point of damage to the target, or you daze the target for one round, during which time the difficulty of all its tasks is modified by one step to its detriment (your choice). If you daze the target in conjunction with another ability that dazes (such as a vector's Bash), the target is instead stunned, unable to move or act for a round. Enabler.

Shadow. The difficulty of your attack with a medium or smaller weapon is reduced by one step. Enabler.

Tier 2: Flurry (2+ Speed points). You make an extra melee attack, but the difficulty of the extra attack is increased by one step. If you choose to apply Effort, each level applied grants you another extra attack that is one step more difficult. For example, if you use Flurry and apply two levels of Effort, you can make four attacks. Roll for the first attack normally. The difficulty of the second attack is increased by one step, the difficulty of the third is increased by two steps, and the difficulty of the fourth is increased by three steps. Enabler.

Tier 3: Learning the Way. You can choose from one of two benefits. Either you are trained in using medium and smaller melee weapons in which you are not already trained (including your own body), or you inflict 2 additional points of damage when making melee attacks with Elemental Fist. Enabler.

Wuxia Leap (5 Speed points). You can leap to a location within short range and make a melee attack at any point along that path as part of the same action. If your preferred element is chi, you can leap within long range.

Tier 4: Elemental Skin (4 Speed points). When you wish it, your body exudes an aura of your chosen element for up to ten minutes, which has the following effect. Action to initiate.

Chi. You gain +1 to your Speed Edge.

Fire. A foe who makes a successful melee attack against you catches on fire and burns as if struck by your fiery Elemental Fist.

Lightning. Fields of electricity and magnetism absorb a portion of attacks made against you. You gain +1 to Armor.

Shadow. You're hard to make out. Attacks

Bash, page 26

against you are modified by one step to the attacker's detriment.

Tier 5: Mastering the Way (4 Speed points). When using Elemental Fist, you can reroll any attack roll you wish and take the better of the two results. Enabler.

Tier 6: Elemental Ride (5 Speed points). When you use Elemental Skin, you can enhance the manifestation to gain additional mobility. If you manifest fire or lightning, you can fly for ten minutes, moving a long distance each round. If you manifest shadow, you can step between shadows you can see within long range without moving through the space separating them. And if you manifest chi, you can run a long distance each round, ignore obstacles of level 4 or lower by "free running" over them, and carry one other creature of your size or smaller with you. Action to initiate; action to move.

NAMES

You are a namer. You can discern someone's common, given name (such as Jack, Chihiro, or Sebastian) merely by looking at him, and with practice, you can also learn that person's true, hidden name. Knowing a person's hidden name gives you power over him. As mastery comes, you can eventually hide someone's name, know his thoughts, or even change his name, and with it, his form. To be a namer is to be a force of creation and change, though some walk a darker path and attempt to erase the names of everyone and everything that displeases them.

You tend to wear a guise that doesn't look entirely human, perhaps because you are a master of disguise, because you use masks to manifest your magic, or because you're truly not fully human in the recursion where you become a namer.

Spinners are the most likely character types to be namers, but the focus has almost equal draw for paradoxes.

Connection: If this is your starting focus, choose one of the following connections.

1. Pick one other PC. That character borrowed an important book from you and has never returned it.

2. Pick one other PC. You gave her a short rhyme that brings good dreams when she says it before she sleeps, but you wonder if the nightmares are building up in the dark.

3. Pick one other PC. You're pretty sure that a name you made up out of the blue summoned that character into existence some time ago. If the PC knows that you believe this, he might think you're full of yourself, think you're crazy, or possibly believe it himself.

4. Pick one other PC. She asked you for a name that would allow her to stand up to a cruel authority figure. You told her you'd find the perfect name for her need, but you're having trouble with the syllables.

Equipment: Scholar's clothes, quill and ink, reference book, notebook, a weapon of your choice, and 30 crowns.

Names GM Intrusions: *A named target attacks you instead of standing calm or doing as you command. A named law of reality bends differently than you expected. A named object breaks from stress or explodes. You forget your own name for a round and stand unable to take an action.*

Minor Effect Suggestion: You learn a deeply buried secret the target was trying to hide.

Major Effect Suggestion: Foes within short range are dazed for one round upon hearing you speak a hidden name. During this time, the difficulty of all tasks they perform is modified by one step to their detriment.

Tier 1: Name (1 Intellect point). You attempt to discern the common, given name of a person, creature, or object within short range. This ability doesn't give you power over the target, but it does allow you to address the target by name or potentially learn the real identity of someone in disguise or the common name of an odd object. Knowing the name of a person who hasn't revealed it to you could provide an asset to your attempts to persuade, fool, intimidate, or ingratiate yourself with the target, depending on the situation. Action.

Onomatology. You are trained in the origin, history, and use of names. Enabler.

Tier 2: Steal Name (2 Intellect points). You steal the name of a target within short range by lifting it directly from the creature's thoughts. An affected target ceases taking actions for up to one minute as it attempts to recall its name, or for as long as you use your action each round to concentrate on hiding the name from it. If the target is attacked, endangered, or seriously provoked, it stops worrying about its name and acts normally. Action.

Name Meld (1 Intellect point). When you successfully use Steal Name on a target, you also read the target's surface thoughts at the same time, even if the target tries to prevent you from doing so. You can continue to read the target's surface thoughts for as long as you keep its name hidden from it by using Steal Name (up to one minute). Enabler.

Tier 3: Anti-Name (3+ Intellect points). You speak a name that is antithetical to up to three targets within long range. The Anti-Name inflicts 2 points of damage that ignore Armor. For each level of Effort you apply, you can choose to attack an additional target. Action.

Tier 4: Name Object or Force (4+ Intellect points). Your study of names goes beyond creatures and extends to objects and even the laws of reality. Objects become more cooperative and laws bend to your aid when you name them, and the difficulty of a task you attempt is reduced by two steps. For example, if you name a level 4 wall prior to attempting to climb it, you treat the climb as a level 2 task. If you try to jump across a gap between cloud ships and name the local force of gravity, a difficulty 5 Might-based task becomes difficulty 3.

For each 2 additional Intellect points you spend, the difficulty of the task decreases by one additional step. Enabler.

Tier 5: Command Name (6+ Intellect points). If you've previously used Steal Name on a target, you can attempt to control the target's actions if it is within short range and can hear and understand you. If you succeed, you control the target's actions for two rounds by verbal command. Instead of applying Effort to decrease the difficulty, you can apply Effort to increase the duration of control; each level applied extends the duration of Command Name by one round. When the effect ends, the target recalls being under your control unless you prevent that by succeeding on an Intellect-based attack whose difficulty is equal to the target's level. Action to initiate.

Tier 6: Change Name (7+ Intellect points). If you've previously used Steal Name on a target, you can attempt to transform the target into a natural animal by changing its true name. The target must be level 2 or lower. The effect is permanent unless you later return the creature's true name to it as an action, leave the recursion for longer than three days, or die. Instead of applying Effort to decrease the difficulty, you can apply Effort to increase the maximum level of the target. Thus, to change the form of a level 5 target (three levels above the normal limit), you must apply three levels of Effort.

The form you change the target into must be that of a natural wild animal, and its mass can't be more than double the original creature's size. On the other hand, you can reduce a large target down to something as small as your fist. For instance, you could turn a giraffe into a duck, or a human into a turtle. The changed creature isn't under any compulsion to obey you. Over time, its nature may come to suit its new form, as determined by the GM. Action.

NEEDS NO WEAPON

You don't use weapons— you *are* a weapon. With swift knees, kicks, elbows, and submission holds, you inflict incredible damage on your foes. By dint of constant practice and conditioning, you can fight without becoming winded or losing your concentration even when hurt or threatened. Though you like to quip that pain is weakness leaving your body, you probably take great care of yourself, ensuring that your body remains the sharpest, most dependable weapon at your disposal.

MMA fighters or martial artists (as those with your training are sometimes called in recursions that operate under the law of Standard Physics) wear loose, comfortable clothing that allows them a full range of movement. They rarely use weapons other than their own fists, knees, and elbows.

Vectors are the best candidates for making full use of this focus.

Equipment: Street clothes, hand wraps, training knife, energy drink mix, smartphone, multitool with sizeable knife (a light weapon if need be), $250.

Connection: If this is your starting focus, choose one of the following connections.

1. Pick one other PC. He once saw you lose a fight on purpose for money.

2. Pick one other PC. While showing her how to throw someone, you accidentally tore a ligament in her shoulder. She recovered with surgery, but how she feels about you now is up to her.

3. Pick one other PC. In your former circles, his father was known far and wide as something of a minor criminal.

4. Pick one other PC. You think she is a natural and just needs a few pointers on hand-to-hand martial technique. She may feel the same or differently, but you don't plan to give up on her yet.

Minor Effect Suggestion: You flip your opponent over your shoulder, and he lands prone anywhere you select within immediate range.

Major Effect Suggestion: You use a

submission hold on your foe that renders her immobile and unable to take physical actions for one round, plus one additional round if you succeed on a Might- or Speed-based task to maintain the submission.

Tier 1: Fists, Elbows, and Knees of Fury. You inflict 2 additional points of damage with unarmed attacks. Enabler.

Tough As Nails: You have +1 to Armor if you do not wear physical armor. Enabler.

Tier 2: Advantage to Disadvantage (2 Speed points). With a number of quick moves, you make an attack against a foe wielding a weapon, inflicting damage and disarming him so that his weapon is now 10 feet (3 m) away on the ground, or in your hands—your choice. The difficulty of the attack is increased by one step. Action.

Fighting Style: You are trained in unarmed attacks. Enabler.

Needs No Weapon GM Intrusions: *Striking certain foes hurts you as much as it hurts them. Opponents with weapons have greater reach. Complicated martial arts moves can knock you off balance.*

Needs No Weapon is a draggable focus.

Needs No Weapon Equipment:
Ardeyn: *Ardeyn clothing, an explorer's pack, 50 crowns.*
Ruk: *Ruk clothing, an umbilical, light tools, 120 bits.*

Tier 3: Moving Like Water (3 Speed points). You spin and move so that your defense and attacks are aided by your fluid motion. For one minute, the difficulty of your attacks and Speed defense rolls is decreased by one step. Action.

Tier 4: Deflect Attacks (4 Speed points). For one minute, you automatically deflect or dodge any ranged projectile attacks. However, during this time, the difficulty of all other actions in any round where you are attacked by ranged projectiles is increased by one step. Action to initiate.

Tier 5: Stunning Attack (4 Might points). You hit your foe in just the right spot, stunning him so that he loses his next action. This attack inflicts no damage.

Tier 6: Master of Style. You are specialized in unarmed attacks. If you are already specialized in unarmed attacks, you instead deal 2 additional points of damage with unarmed attacks. Enabler.

Negotiates Matters of Life and Death GM Intrusions: *Your luggage is lost. An assassin from a foreign embassy mistakenly targets you. A social faux pas gets the meeting off on the wrong foot. A stomach ailment leads to accidental regurgitation on a foreign dignitary.*

NEGOTIATES MATTERS OF LIFE AND DEATH

You are called upon to deliver messages between heads of state, broker agreements between rival factions, and find a way to bring a swift end to conflict. You're a diplomat, and though you usually attend events as the representative of another power, now and then your skills are the difference between a truce and ongoing bloodshed and war.

You care a lot about your appearance, because how you look is one more tool you can bring to bear when you negotiate. In addition to a good haircut, you wear expensive though understated clothing and stylish shoes. You also carry a briefcase, whether or not it contains important papers.

Spinners make the most obvious diplomats.

Connection: If this is your starting focus, choose one of the following connections.

1. Pick one other PC. Your efforts on that character's behalf secured her a visa, allowing her to escape from a bad situation. Whether she remains grateful or even acknowledges what you did is up to her.

2. Pick one other PC. That character provided vital information you needed to secure a peace deal between two warring states.

3. Pick one other PC. You're pretty sure that your failure to bring two antagonistic factions to an accord is indirectly responsible for the deaths of that character's parents. He knows of your apprehension only if you tell him.

4. Pick one other PC. She asked you to get a friend of hers out of a bad situation abroad. You agreed, but you're still working on the details.

Equipment: Business clothes, passport with valid visas for several foreign states, briefcase, weapon of your choice, smartphone, and $800.

Minor Effect Suggestion: Your entreaty gains an additional small concession, such as the release of a single prisoner.

Major Effect Suggestion: Foes within earshot are dazed for one round after hearing your entreaty. During this time, the difficulty of all tasks they perform is modified by one step to their detriment.

Tier 1: World Traveler. You are trained in finding your way around new places, navigating unfamiliar terrain, and identifying important contacts within a few hours of arriving someplace new. Enabler.

Polyglot. You are practiced in speaking up to four other languages of your choice. Enabler.

Tier 2: Diplomat. You are trained in all tasks related to pleasant social interaction and persuasion. You're also trained in tasks related to detecting falsehoods. Enabler.

Tier 3: Due Diligence. After a ten-hour recovery roll, choose one skill that you believe will clearly help you reach a particular goal. You are trained in tasks related to achieving that goal if you can spend at least an hour going over research materials or otherwise practicing the skill. Enabler.

Tier 4: Command (3 Intellect points). Your audible command, backed by your sheer force of will and charisma, targets a creature within short range that can understand you. An affected creature attempts to carry out your command as its next action. The command can't inflict direct harm on the creature or its allies, so "Commit suicide" won't work, but "Flee" might. In addition, the command can require the creature to take only one action, so "Unlock the door" might work, but "Unlock the door and shoot whoever you see on the other side" won't. If you also have the spinner twist Fast Talk, you *can* command the creature to attempt to harm itself or others as its next action. Action.

Tier 5: Calm (3 Intellect points). Through reasoned discourse, appeals to sanity and the common good, and other entreaties, you prevent a target within long range from attacking anyone or anything for one round. If you also have the spinner twist Enthrall, a target remains calm for one minute after you

use this ability if it or its allies are not attacked. Action.

Tier 6: Call in Favor (4 Intellect points). Lots of people owe you favors, even those employed by or allied with a foe. When you call in a favor successfully, an affected target of level 3 or less within short range does what he can to help you out of a specific fix in a way that minimizes his risk of revealing his divided loyalties to his employer or other allies. For example, he might untie you, slip you a knife, leave a cell door unlocked, and so on. Each additional time you attempt to use this ability, the difficulty increases by one step. The difficulty returns to normal after your next ten-hour recovery roll. Action.

 PILOTS STARCRAFT

You're a crack starship pilot.

You feel most alive when the engines are running hot, the floor plates are thrumming beneath your feet, and the stars (or fractalscapes) stream past the viewports in a continuous accelerating streak. Whether you pilot starcraft along a dangerous trade route, explore places no one has gone before, or work as a courier, you are the master of your own domain: your starship.

Depending on the recursion where this focus is available, your starcraft either moves between discrete locations in a given recursion, *is* a recursion in and of itself, or navigates the Strange. Before you choose this focus, work with your GM to be sure that you'll have the opportunity to access a starcraft or chaos ship.

Piloting is a glamorous job that requires glamorous attire, so you wear striking clothing, possibly including holo-tattoos, data jewelry, and other elaborate accessories.

Spinners are most drawn to this focus, though paradoxes and vectors also enjoy the freedom of piloting a starcraft.

Connection: If this is your starting focus, choose one of the following connections.

1. Pick one other PC. You promised that character a trip anywhere she wanted to go in a starship. She hasn't yet taken you up on your offer.

2. Pick one other PC. You smuggled goods in your starcraft for him in the past, and it ended

Pilots Starcraft GM Intrusions: The starcraft gets lost in space (or in the Strange). The vessel breaks down in the middle of nowhere. Enemy starcraft suddenly appear at the edge of sensor range. You find an alien stowaway.

If you take this focus in Ruk, your starcraft is a chaos ship, and the focus name changes to Sails the Strange.

Fast Talk, page 39

Enthrall, page 39

up entangling you in legal trouble. You've mostly forgotten the incident. Mostly.

3. Pick one other PC. That character confided in you that she suspects you are an agent of an enemy organization. You deny it.

4. Pick one or more other PCs. You accidentally crashed your starcraft when those characters were aboard. Everyone was hurt, and one other former comrade was killed in the incident.

Equipment: Clothing appropriate to your recursion (in Ruk, a bodysuit and an umbilical), a weapon of your choice, an overdrawn account (−300 bits), and, with your GM's approval, access to a small starcraft.

Minor Effect Suggestion: The difficulty of the next task attempted by an ally (either personally or in operating one of the starcraft's systems, such as communication, sensors, weapons, and so on) is reduced by one step.

Major Effect Suggestion: You can take an immediate extra action, either personally or in operating one of the starcraft's systems, such as communication, sensors, weapons, and so on.

All Song, page 192

Small starcraft: level 4; health 20; Armor 4; radically compresses time required to travel distances in normal space by traveling through an alternate medium (such as hyperspace, the Strange, or a warp bubble); attack inflicts 5 points of damage to a range of 20 miles (32 km); fits six people plus cargo

Tier 1: Pilot. You are trained in all tasks related to piloting a starcraft. Generally speaking, piloting tasks are Speed-based tasks, though using sensors and communication instruments are Intellect-based tasks. Enabler.

Flex Lore. After each ten-hour recovery roll when you have access to the starcraft's digital library (or the All Song, if you begin in Ruk), choose one field of knowledge related to a world, a site in the Strange, a recursion, or some other location. The field might be habitations, customs, governments, characteristics of the main race or races, important figures, and so on. You're trained in that field until you use this ability again. You could use this ability with an area of knowledge you're already trained in to become specialized. Enabler.

Tier 2: Salvage and Comfort (2 Intellect points). You're familiar with open space (or the Strange itself). If you spend an hour using your craft's sensors and make a difficulty 3 Intellect roll,

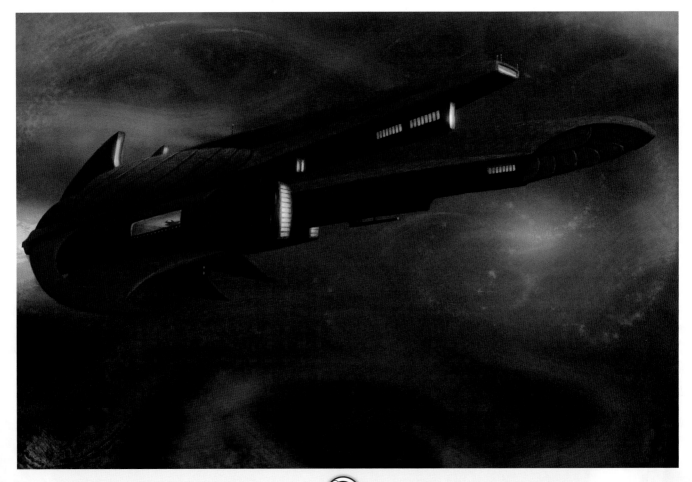

you can find salvage in the form of abandoned spacecraft, drifting motes of matter that were once inhabited, or a place to hide from pursuit in what most people would otherwise assume to be empty space (such as in a nebula, an asteroid field, or the shadow of a moon). Salvage you turn up includes enough food and water for you and several others, as well as the possibility of weapons, clothing, technological artifacts, survivors, or other usable items. In other contexts, this ability counts as training in tasks related to perception. One hour.

Mentally Tough. Staring into the naked weave of hyperspace, the Strange itself, warped space, or a similar effect related to faster-than-light travel is hard on the mind, but you've developed resistance. You're trained in Intellect defense tasks. Enabler.

Tier 3: Expert Pilot. You are specialized in all tasks related to piloting a starcraft. Enabler.

Passing Mechanic. You are trained in tasks related to the repair and maintenance of a starcraft. Enabler.

Tier 4: Sensor Array (3 Intellect points). You are trained in using starcraft sensory instruments. These instruments allow users to answer general questions about a location, such as "How many people are in the mining colony?" or "Where did the other spacecraft crash?" Action.

Pilot Expertise. You add 3 points to your Speed Pool. Enabler.

Tier 5: Like the Back of Your Hand. The difficulty of all tasks directly related to a starcraft that you own or have a direct connection with is decreased by one step. Tasks include repair, refueling, finding a breach in the hull, finding a stowaway, and so on. The same goes for any attack or defense rolls you make within the starcraft against enemy boarders, as well as any attack or defense rolls you make with the ship against enemy ships. Enabler.

Tier 6: Remote Control (5 Intellect points). You can use a starcraft's communication and sensor arrays to launch an attack that briefly renders an enemy starcraft within 20 miles (32 km) inoperative for up to a minute. Action.

Incomparable Pilot. While on a starcraft you own or have a direct connection with, your Might Edge, Speed Edge, and Intellect Edge increase by 1. When you make a recovery roll on a starcraft you're familiar with, you recover an additional 5 points. Enabler.

 ## PROJECTS ENERGY

You can project a particular kind of energy from a custom device you carry (or that is integrated with you) or from your very flesh. When you first gain this focus, you and your GM must choose what kind of energy you emit, and how you emit it. Types of energy include heat, light, sonic, electricity, x-rays, plasma, magnetic pulses, radiation, cold, colored "light" that delivers a massive concussive force, or something else. How you emit the energy depends on whether you project it from a device, from your hands, when you scream, or (a perennial favorite) from your eyes. Whatever your choices, you may be called upon to summon all your energy at once when the world demands sacrifice from a true hero.

You probably wear a colorful (but tough) suit, goggles to protect your eyes from energy discharges, and a utility belt for needful things. If you gain this focus in a Supers recursion, your suit also probably displays your personal emblem, which is tied to your code name.

Paradoxes are especially drawn to this focus because projecting power and energy is something they are already adept at doing, though vectors are also adept at projecting energy as attacks.

Connection: If this is your starting focus, choose one of the following connections.

1. Pick one other PC. She created a device (or a mental exercise) that helps you keep your ability to project energy under control.

2. Pick one other PC. When you first met, you mistook him for someone who needed blasting, and you obliged. He still has a few scars, but whether he forgives you or not is up to him.

3. Pick one or more other PCs. If they agree, you all gained your abilities together during a special event, such as being caught out in a meteor storm, crashing into the back of a vehicle transporting toxic waste, voyaging into the Strange during a freak chaos storm, or something similar.

Projects Energy GM Intrusions: *Your equipment, clothing, or suit is scorched or destroyed. A beam reflects off a surface and hits an unintended target. You ingest too much energy while draining a device and risk going nova unintentionally.*

Supers recursion, page 27

4. Pick one other PC. This character is somehow immune to the energy you emit.

Equipment: A suit (light armor) with integrated smartphone functionality, a weapon of your choice, a utility belt (which includes a holster for your weapon, a flashlight, a wallet with $200, and extra space for cyphers), and salve for burns.

Energy Abilities: If you perform revisions, those that deal damage at long range use the kind of energy that you project. For example, if you use Exception, instead of the target being jolted by a confluence of fundamental forces, it takes damage from your chosen energy, which might be plasma beams, force beams, fire, or something else. As another example, Shatter causes an object to detonate, but in this case, it does so because of the energy you project.

Minor Effect Suggestion: A residue of your energy clings to you, granting you +1 to Armor for one round.

Major Effect Suggestion: Make an immediate Emit Energy attack against a foe that costs only 1 Intellect point.

Exception, page 32

Shatter, page 32

Tier 1: Emit Energy (2 Intellect points). You project a beam of energy at a target within long range that deals 5 points of energy damage. Action.

Suit. You can wear your specially made custom suit (which serves as light armor) for long periods of time without tiring and can compensate for slowed reactions from wearing armor. You reduce the Might cost per hour for wearing armor and the Speed Pool reduction for wearing armor by 2. Enabler.

Tier 2: Energy Sheath (1+ Intellect point). When you wish it, your body is sheathed in a layer of your chosen energy for ten minutes. Your Energy Sheath doesn't hurt you, but it automatically inflicts 2 points of damage to anyone who tries to touch you or strike you with a melee attack. You also gain +2 to Armor against damage from your chosen energy type. For each level of Effort applied, you gain an additional +1 to Armor against damage from your chosen energy. Enabler.

Tier 3: Convert Energy. You can drain the power from a device, allowing you to add 1 point to your Intellect Pool per level of the device. The GM determines whether the device is fully drained (likely true of most handheld or smaller devices, including cyphers) or retains some power (likely true of large machines and artifacts). Action.

Tier 4: Energy Flight (5 Intellect points). You create an aura of your energy that allows you to fly a short distance each round for up to ten minutes. You can't carry other creatures with you. Action to initiate.

Tier 5: Energy Detonation (5+ Intellect points). You charge a small object (such as a plate, a coffee cup, a book, or a rock) with your energy so that it literally glows, vibrates, or steams (depending on your energy type). As part of the same action, you can either hurl the object at a target within short range, or carefully set it down and designate a time within the next minute when it will explode. Whether it explodes on impact or at the designated time, all creatures within immediate range take 4 points of damage. If you apply Effort to increase the damage, the explosion deals 2 additional points of damage per level applied (instead of 3 points); however, targets in the area take 1 point of damage even if you fail the attack roll. Action.

Tier 6: Energy Nova (7 Intellect points). You can build up energy and release it in a miniature nova that targets all creatures and objects within short range (roll attacks for each creature individually). Each round you spend building up energy as your action adds 5 points of damage to the amount of energy you eventually release; however, in each round you must apply one more level of Effort than you applied in the previous round (no Effort in round 1, one level of Effort in round 2, two levels of Effort in round 3, and so on). For example, if you spend three rounds building up energy and apply two levels of Effort, you inflict 15 points of damage when you go nova in round 4. One or more actions to build up energy; action to release.

REJUVENATES THE INFIRM

You attended the best medical academy and got top marks in your class. You completed your internship in the Tissue Restoratorium in only a year. Now that you have finally achieved your medical honors and received your personal autodoc (slaved to your nervous system), you have your pick of appointments. You can choose to apply your arts almost anywhere, or if you choose, put your skills to use out in the field. Doing the latter is more dangerous, but you're likely to find subjects in more immediate need of your talents.

You probably wear clothes that bear the insignia of a medical professional, and when people address you by your honorific ("Doctor," in most recursions), you approve.

Spinners are more often than not the kind of characters that choose this focus.

Connection: If this is your starting focus, pick one of the following connections.

1. Pick one other PC. You failed to heal that character once, and she nearly lost her life.

2. Pick one other PC. When you rebuild that character's tissue, he gains 1 additional point.

3. Pick two other PCs. To fully regenerate one, you had to use your autodoc to remove an extra organ from the other.

4. Pick one other PC. Your attempt to heal that character's deathly ill relative ended in the patient's sudden demise.

Equipment: Clothing appropriate to your recursion (in Ruk, a bodysuit and an umbilical), an autodoc (slaved to your nervous system), a weapon of your choice, and an account with 200 bits.

Minor Effect Suggestion: The target is healed for 1 additional point.

Major Effect Suggestion: The target is healed for 2 additional points.

Tier 1: Rebuild Tissue (1 Intellect point). Using your handheld autodoc, you restore 1d6 points to one stat Pool of any creature. This ability is a difficulty 2 Intellect task. Each time you attempt to heal the same creature, the difficulty increases by one step. The difficulty returns to 2 after that creature rests for ten hours. Action.

Tier 2: Regeneration Pool (2+ Intellect points). Using your handheld autodoc, you grant

Rejuvenates the Infirm
GM Intrusions: *Your autodoc needs a charge. Your autodoc malfunctions and severs one of the subject's limbs. The subject lapses into a coma for no apparent reason. A relative of a subject you failed to save in the past appears and demands reparations.*

a creature an additional stat Pool called Regeneration that contains 1 point. Creating the Pool is a difficulty 2 Intellect task. Each time you attempt to grant an additional point to the same creature's Pool, the difficulty increases by one step and you must apply an additional level of Effort (no Effort to grant 1 point, one level of Effort to grant 2 points, and so on). The difficulty returns to 2 after that creature rests for ten hours. The Regeneration Pool lasts until it is used up or until after that creature's next ten-hour recovery roll, whichever comes first. When spending points from any other Pool, the creature can take one, some, or all of the points from the Regeneration Pool first. Action.

Tier 3: Alleviate (3 Intellect points). Using your handheld autodoc, you attempt to cancel or cure one malady (such as disease or poison) in one creature that you touch. Action.

Tier 4: Reprogram Mind (4+ Intellect points). Using your handheld autodoc, you attempt to deprogram a creature whose mind has been suborned by an outside influence. A creature that doesn't want to be deprogrammed must first be restrained. You can also use this ability to inject attitudes and memories into a level 2 or lower creature that didn't originally have those attitudes or memories. Subtle memories and attitudes could be permanent, but radical changes to a creature's mind usually last a day at most. Instead of applying Effort to decrease the difficulty, you can apply Effort to increase the maximum level of the target. Thus, to adjust the mind of a level 5 target (three levels above the normal limit), you must apply three levels of Effort. Action.

Tier 5: Increase Edge (5 Intellect points). Using your handheld autodoc, you can give a creature +1 to its Might Edge, Speed Edge, or Intellect Edge for up to one hour, or until you use this ability again. This ability is a difficulty 3 Intellect task. Action.

Tier 6: Nanobot Revival (6+ Intellect points). Using your handheld autodoc, you can bring a dead creature back to life if you have, at minimum, its mostly intact brain. The target's missing tissues are rebuilt from surrounding matter until a fully restored, living creature is revived after twenty-four hours. This ability is a difficulty 4 Intellect task. Each time you attempt to return the same creature to life, the difficulty increases by one step. Action to initiate; twenty-four hours to revive.

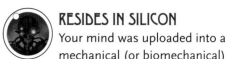

RESIDES IN SILICON

Your mind was uploaded into a mechanical (or biomechanical) droid no larger than a grapefruit; you're a probe droid. You can hover about and sense the world with electronic senses, or interface directly with networked systems. You are more fragile than your companions and less adept at purely

physical tasks, but your ability to scan and analyze reality is second to none, and as you grow more practiced in your mechanical shell, you learn to take over other systems, eventually creating brief duplicate instances of your consciousness that you can use to infect enemy machines and networked systems.

Your mechanical body is probably a hovering sphere the size of a human fist, leaking digital light from external circuits and scan ports.

Paradoxes and spinners are most effective as probe droids, since many of their mental abilities (and attacks) do not suffer the deficit that physical tasks do when attempted by a tiny robotic form.

Connection: If this is your starting focus, choose one of the following connections.

1. Pick one other PC. He was the one who found and activated you in the detritus of some past conflict you can't recall.

2. Pick one other PC. Until you woke to who you really were, she deployed you as a scanning tool. Now that you're a fully functional entity,

you're not yet sure how you feel about having been treated as a simple tool for so long.

3. Pick one other PC. When something catastrophic happened to your original flesh body, his intervention was partly responsible for uploading your mind into a probe droid. You're not sure if you're thankful or resentful about how things turned out.

4. Pick one other PC. She knows who you were before you were uploaded even if no one else does.

Equipment: Yourself (and an attached umbilical, if in Ruk) and an account with 80 bits.

Minor Effect Suggestion: The difficulty of the next action you attempt is decreased by one step.

Major Effect Suggestion: Your tiny droid body darts behind your foe's ally, and the foe attacks its ally instead of you.

Tier 1: Ghost in the Machine. You mind has been uploaded into a miniature quantum digital

Resides in Silicon GM Intrusions: *A detonation hurls your droid body a long distance (in addition to any other effects). Anti-intrusion digital protection attacks you as you attempt to interface with something. An enemy's successful attack grabs your droid body.*

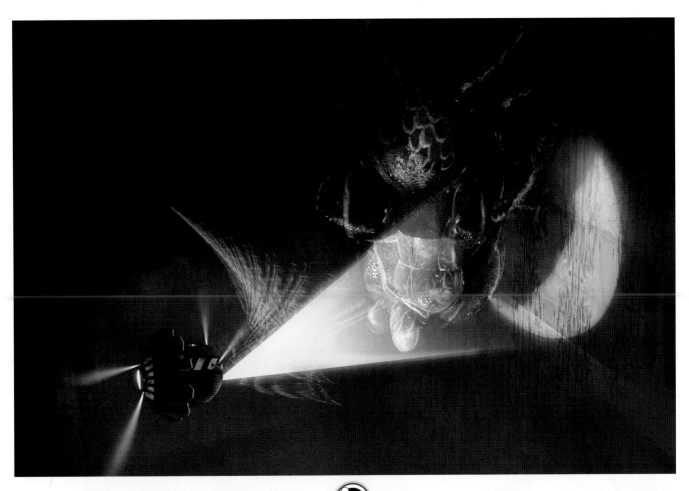

chip embedded in a tiny hovering droid about 5 inches (13 cm) in diameter. You retain your Speed Pool, Intellect Pool, and special abilities (work with your GM if an ability provided by your descriptor or type requires additional translation). Your Might Pool is reduced by 5 points. You have no equipment—you *are* your equipment. Your cyphers translate into your new form as internal digital engrams you can call upon as your action. As a probe, you have a limited ability to affect the physical world. You move by levitating to a maximum height of 6 feet (2 m) over the ground. The difficulty of all physical tasks (other than fine manipulation) is increased by two steps because you must accomplish them with manipulators made of projected hard light. Most mental tasks, including certain tasks and attacks granted by revisions and twists, are not penalized. Because of your size, foes often ignore you, and you're hard to hit: the difficulty of your stealth tasks and defense rolls is decreased by one step.

Interface. By directly plugging a filament (in Ruk, an umbilical) into a device, you can identify it and communicate with it (if it is capable of interaction). This communication doesn't grant you any special abilities (but see Controlling Interface). Enabler.

Illumination (1 Intellect point). You can project bright light in a cone that extends a short distance. Enabler.

Tier 2: Scan and Analyze (3 Intellect points). You can analyze objects and areas within immediate range to learn a surprising amount of information from tiny scraps of evidence. To do so, you must spend one minute scanning an object or area. Once you finish scanning, you can discover up to three pertinent pieces of information about the object or area, possibly clearing up a lesser mystery and pointing the way to solving a greater one. The GM will decide what you learn and what the level of difficulty is to learn it. (For comparison, pulling a partly degraded piece of stored data from a derelict robot is a difficulty 3 task for you.) One minute to scan.

Tier 3: Controlling Interface (5+ Intellect points). You lock on to a machine or biomechanical device and control it as if it were your body

for one hour. The target must be level 2 or lower. To lock on to a resisting machine, you must succeed on a physical attack. Once you have established control, you sense what the machine senses. You can allow it to act freely or override its control on a case-by-case basis. Instead of applying Effort to decrease the difficulty, you can apply Effort to increase the maximum level of the target. Thus, to control a level 5 machine (three levels above the normal limit), you must apply three levels of Effort. When the effect ends, the machine has no record of having been controlled or anything it did while under your command, unless you wish it to. Action to initiate.

Tier 4: Holographic Presence (4 Intellect points). You project a hard light hologram of a physical body resembling the person you were before you were uploaded into a probe droid. The hologram lasts for one hour and either surrounds your tiny droid form or appears somewhere within long range of your droid body. The hologram is dressed however you wish and looks real to general scrutiny, but a close look reveals its ephemeral nature. The hologram can manipulate objects better than your hard-light manipulators can; the difficulty of all physical tasks is not increased by two steps. You must spend your action each round to control the hologram or it freezes in the last position you gave it, and you must remain within long range to control the hologram. If you form the hologram around your droid body, it grants you +1 to Armor. Action to initiate.

Tier 5: Network Injection (5 Intellect points). When you have access to an interlinked communication web (such as the All Song in Ruk), you can inject your consciousness into it. Once you do, you can spend one minute to identify and attempt to communicate with any or all machines, including biomechanical machines, within 10 miles (16 km) that are also connected directly or wirelessly. You can ask one basic question about the machines or anything happening near them and receive a simple answer. For example, while in an area with many machines, you could ask "Where is the chrysalid?" and if the creature is within 10 miles (16 km) of you, one or more machines

If an uploaded character acquires a new cypher, the cypher is digitized and uploaded as an engram into the probe body as an action. The droid can also drop an unused cypher, at which point it coalesces into existence from a swirl of fractal light.

All Song, page 192

will probably provide the answer. While you communicate with the system, your droid body is inactive, and you are unaware of what is happening to it or in its vicinity. One minute to initiate.

Tier 6: Another Instance of You (6 Intellect points). When you have access to an interlinked communication web (such as the All Song in Ruk) or a willing machine, you can inject another instance of your consciousness into it that lasts up to one hour. The additional instance of you has your abilities but performs all tasks as a level 5 creature. The instance lasts until its health is depleted, an hour elapses, you use this ability again, or the host system is destroyed. Action to initiate.

SCULPTS LIGHT

You are a master sculptor, but your medium is translucent light. Hard as iron when fashioned, your creations fade to nothing when you dismiss them. Your ability might come from an object you built or found, be an inborn gift, be the product of an advanced psychic talent, or derive from something far stranger. Objects you create from hard light possess a color distinctive to you, and they are bright enough to create dim light within immediate range of each manifestation. Do you consider your gift a weighty responsibility or the means to accomplish your own ends?

You often wear clothing that matches the chosen color of your constructs. If you take this focus in a Supers recursion, your clothing might be a suit that also displays your personal emblem, which is tied to your code name.

Spinners and paradoxes are the most likely characters to choose Sculpts Light.

Connection: If this is your starting focus, choose one of the following connections.

1. Pick one other PC. The character chose your heroic-sounding code name for you.

2. Pick one other PC. You tend to forget that character's code name and call her by her real

Supers recursion, page 27

Sculpts Light GM Intrusions: *Your hard light construct winks out unexpectedly. The light of a construct gives you away. Someone with light-based powers of an opposing color appears and announces himself as your nemesis.*

name, even on missions where it's important to keep your true identities hidden.

3. Pick one other PC. That character is somehow directly responsible for your powers. Perhaps he designed the experiment that led to the accident, he gave you the object that pulses with hard light potential, or something else.

4. Pick one other PC. She asked you to design a hard light sculpture of her father that wouldn't degrade when you left the area. You're still working on it.

Equipment: Clothing appropriate to your recursion (in Ruk, a bodysuit and an umbilical; in a Supers recursion, a suit and a utility belt) and an account with 70 bits.

Minor Effect Suggestion: Your construct blazes with extra light intensity, partly blinding your target on its next turn, which modifies any task it attempts by one step to its detriment.

Major Effect Suggestion: Make an immediate extra attack with your Hard Light Limb ability.

Hard light limb: level 3; moves a long distance; inflicts 4 points of damage

Tier 1: Hard Light Limb (3 Intellect points). You can produce an additional arm, either connected to your body or floating freely in space up to a long distance away. You can make it look like your normal arm, like the limb of a creature you've seen or encountered, like a simple geometric grasping surface, or like another shape you and your GM agree upon. In all cases, the arm is composed of translucent light of your chosen color. It acts as you direct, floating in the air. Directing the arm is an action. Without a command, the arm does nothing. It can move a long distance in a round, but it never moves farther than long range away from you. The arm's hand can grab, move, and carry things. The arm can also attack. Once created, the arm lasts for ten minutes. Action to create; action to direct.

Tier 2: Hard Light Blast (1+ Intellect point). You can project blasts of hard light that inflict 3 points of damage on a target within short range. Instead of applying Effort to reduce the difficulty or increase damage, you can apply Effort to increase the range by 100 feet (30 m) per level applied. Action.

Hard Light Shell (1 Intellect point). When you wish it, your body is covered in a flexible, translucent shell of light that gives you +1 to Armor. The shell lasts for ten minutes. Enabler.

COLOR OF LIGHT CONSTRUCTS

As presented, the Sculpts Light focus doesn't suggest a color for the light produced by the wielder. Depending on the recursion where the focus is offered, the color choice might be an important aspect of character creation. If you and your GM wish, you can choose a color from the visible spectrum. This light choice could associate your character with a group of NPCs who wield that same color of light, if such a group exists in the campaign. For instance, if you choose violet, your character might be part of an organization called the Ultraviolets whose members pride themselves on lucid, mindful interaction with the world. If your GM agrees, you also gain color-related effects while your focus is active. The following list provides some ideas, but your GM might come up with a different set of effects for each color, or other colors entirely.

Red: The color of danger and heat. When you use Hard Light Blast, you can choose that the damage you deal comes from the burning quality of your light.

Yellow: The color of optimism—or sometimes optimism's opposite, fear. When you use Hard Light Blast, you can choose to frighten the target instead of dealing damage. All tasks, attacks, and defenses of the target are modified by one step to its detriment for a couple of rounds.

Green: The color of growth and renewal. The difficulty of all healing tasks you attempt is decreased by one step, and you can attempt a healing task within long range by targeting an ally with your light.

Blue: The color of sadness and cold. When you use Hard Light Blast, you can choose that the damage you deal comes from the freezing quality of your light.

Violet: The color of purity and lucidity. The difficulty of all tasks related to using calm reason to reach a conclusion is decreased by one step. When you use Hard Light Blast, the damage you deal is considered to be mental trauma on your target.

Tier 3: Hard Light Object (4 Intellect points). You create a hard light object of any shape you can imagine that is your size or smaller. This is a difficulty 2 Intellect-based task. The object is crude and can have no moving parts, so you can make a sword, a shield, a short ladder, and so on. The hard light object has the approximate mass of the real object, if you choose. Your hard light objects are as strong as iron, but if you do not remain within long range of them, they function for only one minute before fading away. Action.

    Practiced Construct Creator. You add 2 points to your Intellect Pool. Enabler.

Tier 4: Hard Light Armor. When you use Hard Light Shell, you create an airtight internal environmental recycling system within the shell that allows you to survive at oceanic depths or in vacuum for up to three days at a time. Enabler.

    Improved Hard Light Limb: Your hard light limb is a level 4 creature that can be up to double your size. Enabler.

Tier 5: Hard Light Conveyance (6+ Intellect points). You create a level 2 conveyance of hard light that can fly, drive, or dive beneath water for one hour, with you as a passenger. This is a difficulty 2 Intellect-based task. The conveyance can be a simple geometric platform or resemble a vehicle you are familiar with. If you create a vehicle that encases you, you gain +1 to Armor while inside it. For each additional level of Effort applied, you can increase the size of the conveyance so it's large enough to hold additional creatures your size or smaller. In terms of overland movement, your conveyance moves about 20 miles (32 km) per hour and is not affected by terrain if the vehicle is an aircraft or a submersible. You can use Hard Light Armor in conjunction with this ability to provide an airtight internal environment in your conveyance. Action to initiate.

Tier 6: Massive Hard Light Object (7+ Intellect points). You create a hard light object, whose base size can fit within a 10-foot (3 m) cube, floating freely in space up to a long distance away. This is a difficulty 2 Intellect-based task. The object is crude and can have no moving parts, so you can make a wall segment, a block, a box, a massive hammer, and so on. The hard light object has the approximate mass of the real object, if you choose. Your hard light objects are as strong as iron, but if you do not remain within long range of them, they function for only one minute before fading away. If you apply Effort to increase the size of the object, each level applied increases the size by an additional 10-foot (3 m) cube. Action.

    Incredible Hard Light Limb. Your hard light limb is a level 5 creature that can be up to triple your size. You can use it to wield a weapon created with Massive Hard Light Object to attack all creatures within immediate range of each other (one attack roll per creature). Enabler.

 ## SERVES AND PROTECTS

You're a cop. It's a hard job, one that's often thankless, especially when the bad apples among you abuse their authority. But you take it seriously and try to shrug off bad press. It's your job to enforce the law, protect people and property, and keep the peace. Investigating crimes means questioning witnesses and suspects. Often, hard questions are all that's required to get someone to confess. With your badge and your commanding presence, you're perfect for the job.

    While on duty, you are in uniform, display your badge prominently, and carry a gun on your duty belt. When off duty, you wear civvies but still usually carry your gun and badge.

    Cops draw vectors into their ranks, as well as spinners who yearn for the institutional authority a badge brings.

    Connection: If this is your starting focus, choose one of the following connections.

    1. Pick one other PC. That character was once a cadet who trained under you but has now gone his own way.

    2. Pick one other PC. You know she spent several months behind bars, but you're not sure for what.

    3. Pick one other PC. He's an old friend who hates the fact that you're a cop and sometimes tries to get you to quit the force.

    4. Pick one other PC. You know there's a warrant for her on record, probably for unpaid parking fines (though you're not sure). You've

---

Incredible hard light limb: *level 5; moves a long distance; inflicts 6 points of damage*

Improved hard light limb: *level 4; moves a long distance; inflicts 5 points of damage*

Serves and Protects GM Intrusions: *Your gun jams. The car runs out of gas. A suspect decides not to cooperate. A witness reacts badly to seeing your badge and attacks.*

chosen not to question her about it, but you could change your mind later.

Equipment: Police uniform and duty belt (containing handcuffs, radio, holster, and flashlight), a badge, a medium gun and a light bashing weapon, a smartphone, and $200.

Minor Effect Suggestion: The next time you attempt to command the same foe, the difficulty of the task is decreased by one step.

Major Effect Suggestion: The foe either surrenders or is influenced by your ability for twice as long as normal.

Tier 1: Badge. You're an officer of the law and have a badge, even when you're off duty or on sabbatical. When you show it (or a similar facsimile), your badge and your air of authority together give you an asset on all interactions with law-abiding citizens, but this could increase the difficulty of interactions with scofflaws by one step. Enabler.

Practiced With Guns. You are practiced with

○ ● ○

BADGE
Having a real badge requires ongoing employment by a police department. That said, you could be on a sabbatical, taking a leave from active duty, or simply on vacation for several weeks each year without fear of losing your standing. If your police badge is confiscated for any reason and you use a facsimile to gain the benefit of having a badge, there's a chance that someone will recognize it as a fraud (though most NPCs remain snowed).

● ○ ○

using guns and suffer no penalty when using them. Enabler.

Tier 2: Command (3 Intellect points). Calling on your authority as a vested officer of the law, you issue a simple command to a single living creature, which attempts to carry out your command as its next action. The creature must be within short range and able to hear and understand you. The command can't inflict direct harm on the creature or its allies, so "Commit suicide" won't work, but "Flee" might. In addition, the command can require the creature to take only one action, so "Unlock the door" might work, but "Unlock the door and run through it" won't. Action.

Driver. You are practiced with all tasks relating to driving a car. Enabler.

Tier 3: Cool Under Fire. You are trained in Speed defense tasks. Enabler.

Tier 4: Police Training. You are trained in stealth, perception, and picking locks. Enabler.

Tier 5: Commanding Presence (2 Intellect points). You can use this ability in one of two ways.

First, your words keep the attention of up to five NPCs (target each one individually with an Intellect-based attack) who can hear and understand you. This lasts for as long as you speak, up to one minute, but only if the NPCs aren't attacked during that time. If your words are meant to distract the NPCs from noticing other nearby activity, the difficulty of any perception tasks performed by the NPCs is modified by one step to their detriment. If you also have the spinner twist

Enthrall, you can target a group of up to ten NPCs.

Second, your words inspire all friendly NPCs of your choosing who can hear and understand you. For the next hour, they function as if they were one level higher. Action to initiate.

Tier 6: Mentally Tough. You can't let stress or a confusing situation get in the way of making a life-or-death decision. You are trained in Intellect defense tasks. Enabler.

　　Precise Shot. You gain +1 to your Speed Edge.

 ## SMITES THE WICKED

You are a champion of righteousness in a land threatened by evil. You've sworn to uphold a moral cause even if most hope for goodness is dead. Finding the wicked where they hide, especially creatures born into evil or entities whose mere existence is anathema to virtue, is a duty you do not shirk, even on days when you'd rather do anything else. By pledging yourself to the cause of all that's holy, your strength is magnified, your abilities are enhanced, and your purpose is aligned to the divine.

If you are in Ardeyn, the evil threatening the land is the Maker's betrayal and the long absence of the Incarnations. Despite that, the Seven Rules remain bound to the land, and you draw your abilities from that bedrock of moral certainty. The Seven Rules (and the Seven Incarnations, who the rules were named after) are: Commerce, Death, Desire, Law, Lore, Silence, and War.

You probably wear gleaming plate armor, carry a shield with the sigils of the Incarnations inscribed on its surface, and wield a shining shamshir (a blade like a scimitar).

Vectors commonly choose to become sacred warriors who serve a higher power, calling, or sworn oath.

Connection: If this is your starting focus, choose one of the following connections.

1. Pick one other PC. She is the true friend whose belief in a higher power caused you to become the sacred warrior you are today.

Enthrall, page 39

Seven Rules of Ardeyn, page 56

Seven Incarnations of Ardeyn, page 162

Smites the Wicked GM Intrusions: *The demon possesses unexpected additional abilities. Your weapon breaks. A difficult moral choice must be made. Circumstances lead you to have a moment of doubt.*

Whether or not she still believes with the same fervor is up to her.

2. Pick one other PC. That character has made a few offhand comments that make you suspect that he does not hold your cause to be especially sacred.

3. Pick one other PC. This character once talked you through the aftermath of a situation in which you had to make a choice when there was no good choice to be made.

4. Pick one other PC. You want to win him over to your cause. It's up to him whether he's receptive to your pitch.

Equipment: Plate armor, shield, one medium or light melee weapon of your choice, a talisman signifying your cause, and 50 crowns.

Minor Effect Suggestion: A blaze of righteous power causes your foe to drop its weapon and fall to its knees.

Major Effect Suggestion: Your foe has a change of heart, at least for a round, and runs from your righteous might.

Tier 1: Sense the Wicked (2 Intellect points). You sense the presence of the nearest creature of irredeemable evil (such as demons, many dragons, spirits of wrath, and creatures of the Strange like kray, inklings, other Strangers, and other creatures your GM determines) within short range. If the wicked creature has taken special precautions to hide its identity, determining its presence or true nature is an Intellect-based task whose difficulty is equal to the creature's level or the level of the effect employed. Action.

Sacrifice of the Righteous. You can spend points from either your Speed Pool or your Intellect Pool when applying levels of Effort to increase your weapon damage. In addition, you can spend points from either your Might Pool or your Speed Pool when applying levels of Effort to any Intellect-based special ability granted by this focus. Enabler.

Tier 2: Sacred Warrior. You inflict 2 additional points of damage when fighting demons, evil spirits, evil dragons, and Strangers. Enabler.

Hands of the Healer. You are trained in all healing tasks. In addition, when you successfully heal a creature, it regains 2 additional points. Enabler.

A Stranger is the term for any creature native to the Strange, rather than Earth or a recursion.

Tier 3: Trained Warrior. You are trained in using a weapon of your choice in which you are not already trained: light bashing, light bladed, light ranged, medium bashing, medium bladed, medium ranged, heavy bashing, heavy bladed, or heavy ranged. Enabler.

Tier 4: Call Upon the Sacred Incarnations. As a warrior sworn to the memory of the absent Incarnations, you can call upon their influence to cleanse the land of evil. Choose one Incarnation. You gain the associated ability described below.

Commerce. You are trained in detecting the deceptions of other creatures. Enabler.

Death (2+ Intellect points). You banish or destroy one demon, spirit, inimical Stranger, or similar creature within short range of level 1 or less. Instead of applying Effort to decrease the difficulty, you can apply Effort to increase the maximum level of the target. Thus, to destroy or banish a level 5 target (four levels above the normal limit), you must apply four levels of Effort. Action.

Desire (3 Intellect points). With a touch, you restore 1d6 points to one stat Pool of any creature. This ability is a difficulty 2 Intellect task. Each time you attempt to heal the same creature, the task difficulty increases by one step. The difficulty returns to 2 after that creature rests for ten hours. Action.

Law (3 Intellect points). In the name of the Incarnations, you prevent a foe that can hear and understand you from attacking anyone or anything for one round. Action.

Lore (3 Intellect points). Choose a creature within short range. The difficulty of a single task (not an attack or defense roll) performed by that creature is reduced by one step. Action.

Silence (3 Intellect points). In silence lies protection. You create a bubble of protection in an immediate radius around you for one minute. The bubble moves with you. The difficulty of all defense rolls for you and all creatures you designate within the bubble is decreased by one step. Action to initiate.

War (2 Intellect points). You inflict 3 additional points of damage as part of one weapon attack. Action.

Tier 5: Phenomenal Warrior. You are specialized in using a weapon of your choice: light bashing, light bladed, light ranged, medium bashing, medium bladed, medium ranged, heavy bashing, heavy bladed, or heavy ranged. If you are already specialized in using that weapon, you deal 2 additional points of damage with it instead. Enabler.

Tier 6: Courageous Warrior. You and all creatures you designate within an immediate distance cannot be frightened by the effects of magic, creature special abilities, or similar sources. Enabler.

Improved Sacred Warrior. You inflict 3 additional points of damage when fighting demons, evil spirits, evil dragons, and Strangers. Enabler.

SOARS ACROSS THE SKY

You have achieved the dream almost everyone yearns for: you can fly. At first, your fledgling power allows you to move at only hovering speed, but even so, you can rise as high as you want and eventually settle on the top of the tallest mountains to watch the sunset. But soon enough your practice pays off, your speed increases, and you can soar through the sky faster than any bird can match, and eventually, any dragon.

You probably wear a sleek suit, one that includes a (tear-away) cape that flares dramatically when you fly and a mask to protect your eyes from the wind. If you choose this focus in a Supers recursion, your suit also displays your personal emblem, which is tied to your spectacular code name; you should choose one before the media chooses it for you.

Paradoxes, vectors, and spinners are equally drawn to this focus, because who doesn't want to be able to fly?

> *"Above the planet on a wing and a prayer,*
> *My grubby halo, a vapour trail in the empty air,*
> *Across the clouds I see my shadow fly*
> *Out of the corner of my watering eye."*
> —Pink Floyd, "Learning To Fly"

Connection: If this is your starting focus, choose one of the following connections.

1. Pick one other PC. He helped you learn to control your power while you were sleeping so that you didn't float away into the night through an open window.

2. Pick one other PC. She mistook you for an enemy and nearly took you out with a cypher. You still have a few scars from the burns.

3. Pick one other PC. She knows the secret of your origin, which you normally keep hidden because it implicates you as the descendent of a particularly infamous foe (who could also fly).

4. Pick one other PC. If you drop this character while flying, he floats safely to the ground due to some side effect of your ability (or his) that you don't fully understand.

Supers recursion, page 27

Soars Across the Sky GM Intrusions: *It's foggy and you can't see where you're going. You run into a mountainside. A brigand on the ground below takes a shot at you with a bow.*

Equipment: Clothing appropriate to your recursion (in Ardeyn, a sleek, qephilim-made suit of sturdy cloth; in a Supers recursion, a suit with a tear-away cape and a utility belt), a weapon of your choice, and 50 crowns.

Minor Effect Suggestion: You fly to a position your foe didn't expect, and its next attack against you is modified by one step to your foe's detriment.

Major Effect Suggestion: You grab hold of your foe, fly up to 20 feet (6 m) away, and drop him off in a new location.

Tier 1: Hover (1 Speed point). You float slowly into the air. As your action, you can concentrate to remain motionless in the air or move up to a short distance, but no more; otherwise, you drift with the wind or with any momentum you have gained. This effect lasts for up to twenty minutes. Action to initiate.

Suit. If you wear your specially made suit (which serves as light armor), you can wear it for long periods of time without tiring and can compensate for slowed reactions from wearing armor. You reduce the Might cost per hour and the Speed Pool reduction for wearing armor by 2. Enabler.

Tier 2: Flight (4+ Speed points). You can fly or float through the air for one hour. In terms of overland movement, you move about 30 miles (48 km) per hour and are not affected by terrain. For each level of Effort applied, you can increase your speed by an additional 30 miles (48 km) per hour. Action to initiate.

Flying Punch. When you make a melee attack while using Flight (whether with your fist, knee, elbow, or a weapon), you deal 1 additional point of damage. Enabler.

Tier 3: Protected Flight (3 Speed points). An invisible energy barrier forms around your skin while you hover or fly. The barrier lasts for ten minutes, during which time the difficulty of all Speed defense tasks is reduced by one step and you gain +1 to Armor. Enabler.

Tier 4: Falling Sky (5+ Speed points). While you hover or fly and are 10 to 200 feet (3 to 61 m) from a foe, you can attack by super-accelerating yourself toward your foe, at the same time

gaining a momentary pulse of protection from your Protected Flight ability. Your impact deals 4 points of damage to the target and 2 points of damage to all creatures and objects within immediate range of the target. If you apply Effort to increase the damage, you deal 2 additional points of damage per level applied (instead of 3 points), and targets in the area take 1 point of damage even if you fail the attack roll. Action.

Tier 5: Winged Touch. When you use Flight, you can affect one additional creature of your size or smaller for each level of Effort applied. You must touch the creature to bestow the power of flight. You direct the other creature's movement, and while flying, it must remain within sight of you or fall. Enabler.

Veteran Flyer. You add 3 points to your Speed Pool. Enabler.

Tier 6: Supersonic Velocity. When you use Flight, your base rate of movement increases to 190 miles (306 km) per hour. For each level of Effort you apply to increase your speed, instead of increasing it by 30 miles (48 km) per hour as described in Flight, you can instead choose to increase your speed by 300 miles (483 km) per hour for one minute. Thus, if you apply two levels of Effort, your Flight speed could increase to 790 miles (1,271 km) per hour for one minute, breaking the sound barrier. Enabler.

 ## SPEAKS FOR THE LAND

You not only speak for the land, you also protect it and the natural creatures and forests that it supports. In that sense, you are the land's champion. You might be part of an ancient priesthood of a select few who are able to commune with the spirits of nature and who call upon the magic of the forest, moon, storm, and beast. In particular, you know how certain long-lived trees are conduits of worldly magic. When lightning falls from the sky, fires rage, or the earth shakes, these elder trees channel that elemental fury into themselves. An event may burn away a limb or blow off bark, but the energy contained within the tree becomes part of the magic of the land—magic that you, in turn, draw upon.

As a speaker for the land, you probably

wear rough, rugged clothing that shows little concern for style. Most of the time, covering yourself in natural smells to keep your scent from spooking wildlife is more important than bathing to be presentable to other humans.

Paradoxes and spinners are drawn to Speaks for the Land, the former because the abilities are in keeping with the kinds of revisions they already practice, and the latter because representing a point of view is something that comes naturally for them.

Connection: If this is your starting focus, choose one of the following connections.

1. Pick one other PC. You found that character lying unconscious in the woods with no memory of how she got there. Without your help, she likely would have died of exposure.

2. Pick one or more other PCs not from the wilderness. You've decided that you will mentor them to become more appreciative of the land and its natural beauty.

3. Pick one other PC. More often than not, that character is accidentally singed, snagged, bitten, or otherwise caught when you use one of your special abilities.

4. Pick one other PC. That character's sibling is responsible for felling a sacred elder tree that was important to you.

Equipment: Clothing fit for the wilderness, a weapon of your choice, enough dried jerky to last a week, a talisman of petrified oak, and 30 crowns.

Minor Effect Suggestion: A hawk or raven attacks your foe's head for one round, during which time the difficulty of all tasks the foe performs is modified by one step to its detriment.

Major Effect Suggestion: A large ferret, eagle, or similar natural creature snags and makes off with a piece of equipment worn or held by your foe.

Tier 1: Seeds of Fury (1 Intellect point). You throw a handful of seeds in the air that ignite and speed toward a target within long range, scratching the air with twisting smoke trails. The attack deals 3 points of damage and catches the target on fire, which inflicts 1 additional point of damage per round for up to a minute or until the target spends an action dousing the flame. Action.

Wilderness Lore. You are trained in wilderness navigation and in identifying plants and creatures. Enabler.

Tier 2: Grasping Foliage (3+ Intellect points). Roots, branches, grass, or other natural foliage in the area snags and holds a foe you designate

within short range for up to one minute. A foe caught in the grasping foliage can't move from its position, and all physical tasks, attacks, and defenses are modified by one step to the victim's detriment, including attempts to free itself. Instead of applying Effort to reduce the difficulty of your attack, you can apply Effort to deal damage with the initial attack. Each level applied inflicts 2 additional points of damage when Grasping Foliage first snags and holds your foe.

You can also use this ability to clear an area of entangling growth in the immediate radius, such as an area of tall grass, thick brush, impenetrable vines, and so on. Action.

Tier 3: Soothe the Savage (3 Intellect points).
You calm a nonhuman beast within 30 feet (9 m). You must speak to it (although it doesn't need to understand your words), and it must see you. It remains calm for one minute or for as long as you focus all your attention on it. The GM has final say over what counts as a nonhuman beast, but unless some kind of deception is at work, you should know whether you can affect a creature before you attempt to use this ability on it. Demons, dragons, very intelligent creatures, and golems are never affected. Action.

Communication (2 Intellect points). You convey a basic concept to a creature that normally can't speak or understand speech. The creature can also give you a very basic answer to a simple question. Action.

Tier 4: Moon Shape (4+ Intellect points).
You change into a monstrous natural beast, such as a wolf, bear, or other terrestrial creature, for up to one hour. If you try to change during daylight hours when you are not deep underground (or otherwise away from the daylight), you must apply a level of Effort. In your new form, you add 8 points to your Might Pool, gain +2 to your Might Edge, add 2 points to your Speed Pool, and gain +2 to your Speed Edge. Reverting to your normal form is a difficulty 2 task. While in beast form, you are prone to fits of rage (triggered by GM intrusion), during which you attack every living creature within short range, and the only way to end the rage is to revert to your normal form. Either way,

after you revert to your normal form, you take a –1 penalty to all rolls for one hour. If you did not kill and eat at least one substantial creature while in beast form, the penalty increases to –2 and affects all your rolls for the next twenty-four hours. Action to change; action to revert.

Tier 5: Insect Eruption (6 Intellect points).
You call a swarm of insects in a place where it is possible for insects to appear. They remain for one minute, and during this time, they do as you command while they are within long range. They can swarm about and modify any or all creatures' task difficulties by one step to their detriment, or you can focus the swarm and attack all targets within immediate range of each other (all within long range of you). The attacking swarm inflicts 2 points of damage per round. You can also command the swarm to move heavy objects through collective effort, eat through wooden walls, and perform other actions suitable for a supernatural swarm. Action to initiate.

Tier 6: Call the Storm (7+ Intellect points).
If you are outside or in a location that has a ceiling at least 300 feet (91 m) above the floor, you summon a boiling layer of lightning-lit, rumbling clouds up to 1,500 feet (457 m) in diameter for ten minutes. During daylight hours, natural illumination beneath the storm is reduced to dim light. While the storm rages, you can spend an action to send a lightning bolt from the cloud to attack a target you can see directly, inflicting 4 points of damage (you can spend Effort normally on each individual lightning bolt attack). Three actions to initiate; action to call down a lightning strike.

STEALS
You're adept at getting into and out of places without anyone realizing it, usually so you can make off with something valuable. You're a thief, though you don't advertise it. Even those who glamorize your profession do so only in the abstract, which is why you're also adept at pretending to be someone who does odd jobs most of the time. Otherwise, some of your friends might not understand.

You prefer clothing that helps you blend into

Steals is a draggable focus.

Steals GM Intrusions:
The target of your thievery returns early. Your forgery is flawed. A roof tile slips under your foot. The item you stole is a fake. You walk into a sting operation.

the night and does not restrict your movement: a black athletic suit is probably your go-to outfit.

Vectors are great burglars, especially the ones who focus on Speed.

Connection: If this is your starting focus, choose one of the following connections.

1. Pick one other PC. The character knows that you supplement your income through thievery and has kept that information private until now.

2. Pick one other PC. You lifted a valuable item from that character but now regret doing so. She doesn't know you have it and may not have missed it—yet.

3. Pick one other PC. That character was able to pay off a debt thanks to money you provided. He doesn't know that you stole something valuable and fenced it to gain those funds.

4. Pick one other PC. Something you stole indirectly got that character fired from her last job. You don't know if you should tell her or keep quiet.

Equipment: Street clothes, black facemask, climbing shoes, bag of climber's chalk, forgery kit, lockpicks, a weapon of your choice, a pen knife, a smartphone, and $2,000.

Minor Effect Suggestion: You get a +1 bonus to Speed defense rolls for one round.

Major Effect Suggestion: Thanks to your fast hands, you are now holding your foe's weapon (if the foe is within immediate distance).

Tier 1: Second-Story Antics. You are trained in climbing, stealth, and lockpicking. Enabler.

Fence. You've developed a network of people who will buy stolen goods from you, though trying to get a fence to buy a particularly hot item (like a firearm) may require some negotiation. Enabler.

Tier 2: Parkour. You can move a long distance each round if you used your previous action and current action only to move. You can move through cityscapes without ever touching the ground by running and jumping between roofs, fire escapes, and building ledges, but when you do so, you move only a short distance each round. You are trained in balancing and catching yourself to avoid falling. Enabler.

Sense Betrayal. You deal with a lot of questionable types and have learned to watch for signs of violence or false statements. You're trained in detecting when someone is lying to you or not providing the whole truth. Action.

Tier 3: Expert Absconder. If you use your action only to move, the difficulty of all Speed defense tasks is reduced by one step. Enabler.

Forgery. You are trained in forgery. However, it is extremely difficult to forge something especially complex without a forgery kit at your disposal. Enabler.

Tier 4: Fine Art of Theft. You are trained in two of the following: stealth, climbing, jumping, lockpicking, disguise, forgery, deceiving, or detecting lies. If you're already trained in the skill you choose, you become specialized instead. Enabler.

Tier 5: Evasion. You can't be good at getting in if you don't survive getting out. You are trained in all defense tasks.

Steals Equipment:
Ardeyn: *Ardeyn clothing (plus a spare set for climbing), sharkskin gloves for climbing, rope, lockpicks, a fish knife, and 200 crowns.*
Ruk: *Ruk clothing, an umbilical, a facemask graft, a lockpicking graft, a weapon of your choice, a knife, and 120 bits.*

Tier 6: Master Thief. You add 5 points to your Speed Pool.

Forget My Name. You've developed an amazing facility for being forgettable. If you interact with a target of level 3 or less and you do not attack it, the target usually forgets having seen you within a few hours. Enabler.

THROWS BOULDERS

You're freakishly strong. Your muscles have muscles, and you're much broader than most of your peers. With a physique like yours, people tend to get out of your way. Sometimes you wish the problems of day-to-day life were as easy as the ones you face when you go on a quest. Finding chairs that won't collapse under you, doorways that admit you without hitting your shoulders, and horses that can carry you are some of the ordinary vexing issues you wish you didn't have to deal with.

Your clothing probably puts your muscles on display, though you wear thick gauntlets to protect your hands when you're lifting and throwing. If you choose this focus in a Supers recursion (where it's called Throws Cars), your clothing is a suit that also displays your personal emblem, which is tied to your code name.

Vectors are most likely to want to throw boulders because Might is already in their wheelhouse.

Throws Boulders GM Intrusions: *The object you lift breaks up in your grip. You weigh more than most people, and you break through the floor. The vehicle you lift has innocent people inside.*

Supers recursion, page 27

A lead sphere 5 inches (13 cm) in diameter weighs about 47 pounds (21 kg), whereas a marble sphere 9 inches (23 cm) in diameter—equal in size to many statue heads in Ardeyn—weighs about 91 pounds (41 kg).

Connection: If this is your starting focus, choose one of the following connections.

1. Pick one other PC. Both of you competed to be the romantic partner of an NPC, but you both lost out to someone else.

2. Pick one other PC. A building fell on him, and you lifted it off—but only after you elicited a promise from him to pay off a small debt you owed at a local tavern.

3. Pick one other PC. You are positive that she was once a storied villain. Why she's posing as someone different now, you're not sure. Maybe she decided to straighten up and fly right, or maybe you're just confused.

4. Pick one other PC. This character and you have developed a routine: you throw him at distant opponents, and he gains a +1 bonus on the melee attack made as part of your combined actions.

Equipment: Leather armor, heavy gauntlets, three 5-inch (13 cm) diameter lead spheres, and 20 crowns.

Minor Effect Suggestion: Your opponent bounces off of you and falls to the ground at your feet.

Major Effect Suggestion: As part of your attack, you grab your foe and throw her to a new position within short range.

Tier 1: Throw Small Boulder (1 Might point). You hurl a weighted object or small boulder—a dense object that weighs 20 to 100 pounds (9 to 45 kg)—at a target within short distance, inflicting 5 points of damage. Applying Effort to deal additional damage means that you're either throwing the object harder or throwing a slightly larger object (in which case, each level of Effort means an additional 10% increase in the size of a given object of the same density). Action, assuming a suitable boulder is at hand.

Tier 2: Outrageous Musculature. You add 3 points to your Might Pool. Enabler.

Tier 3: Lift Large Boulder (3+ Might points). You can pick up an inert object as big as a large boulder (an object that weighs up to about 3,000 pounds, or 1,360 kg) and move it an immediate distance before putting it down on your next turn. You can apply Effort to increase the maximum weight you can lift by 1,000 pounds (454 kg). Thus, to lift an object that weighs 6,000 pounds (2,722 kg), you must apply three levels of Effort. Action to lift object about 3 feet (1 m) above the ground; action to move object and release.

Tier 4: Thunderclap (5+ Might points). You clap your mighty hands together, creating a shock wave that blasts out to short range in an arc that is approximately 50 feet (15 m) wide at the end. This emanation inflicts 4 points of damage. If you apply Effort to increase the damage, you deal 2 additional points of damage per level applied (instead of 3 points); however, targets in the area take 1 point of damage even if you fail the attack roll. Action.

Tier 5: Leap Over Towers (3+ Might points). You can leap between two points that are within 300 feet (91 m). Each level of Effort you apply increases the distance you can leap by 300 feet (91 m). Action.

Improving Strength. You add 2 points to your Might Pool.

Tier 6: Throw Large Boulder (7+ Might Points). You can pick up an inert object as big as a large boulder (an object that weighs up to about 3,000 pounds, or 1,360 kg) and throw it at a target within short range. All creatures and objects within immediate range of the target that fail to evade the object take 7 points of damage, and the target is pinned (difficulty 7 task to get free). If you apply Effort to increase the weight of the object, each level applied increases the weight you can throw by 200 pounds (91 kg), increases the difficulty of a pinned creature's task to get free, and deals 2 additional points of damage (instead of 3 points); however, targets in the area take 1 point of damage even if you fail the attack roll. Action.

WEARS AN IRON SUIT

You possess an amazing suit of superstrong iron-alloy armor powered by advanced technology, including a micro-fission power source. The suit is fitted to you almost perfectly and grants several abilities that far outstrip those of an unaugmented person.

Your powered armor suit is distinctive, covering you from head to foot in its protective embrace. If you choose this focus in a Supers recursion, your suit is likely blazoned with your symbol, which stands for your code name.

Paradoxes are especially drawn to the focus because they are already adept at projecting power and energy; however, vectors appreciate the upgrade the suit provides to their athletic prowess.

Connection: If this is your starting focus, choose one of the following connections.

1. Pick one other PC. You created your suit, or a component of your suit, based on an idea first suggested by that character.

2. Pick one other PC. She's the only one who knows who you are when you're not wearing your suit.

3. Pick one other PC. The power source for your armored suit sometimes interacts with that character's abilities, though usually in a fashion that temporarily shorts out your armor.

4. Pick one other PC. You once cooked her a meal that gave her food poisoning.

Equipment: Powered suit (in Ruk, the suit contains a retractable umbilical) and an account with debt equal to −20 bits.

Armor Abilities: When you perform moves, revisions, or twists that would normally be produced by you, they are instead produced by your armor. For example, an Exception attack is a confluence of fundamental forces, but when you use it, the effect appears to manifest from a special projector on your armor. This alteration changes nothing other than the power's origin.

Minor Effect Suggestion: Your armor's systems learn from your successful actions. You gain a +1 bonus to rolls involving a similar task (such as making attacks against the same foe or operating the same device).

Major Effect Suggestion: Your powered armor performs better than expected, and you gain a +2 bonus to Speed defense rolls for one round.

Tier 1: Spectacular Armor. Your suit is effectively medium armor (+2 to Armor); however, you suffer no Might cost or Speed reduction penalties for wearing it. In addition, your suit grants other benefits: it provides breathable air for up to eight hours and a comfortable environment even in bitter heat, cold, or underwater to a depth of 20,000 feet (6 km); it allows you to see in the dark up to a short

A spherical piece of marble almost 3 feet in diameter (1 m) weighs about 3,000 pounds (1,360 kg); in a Supers recursion, a small to mid-sized car weighs about the same.

Exception, page 32

Wears an Iron Suit GM Intrusions: *Your armor won't come off. Your armor acts under its own power. Your armor suffers a momentary power loss. Civilians or others are scared by the visage of your iron suit.*

distance; and it folds up into a suitcase-sized object when not being worn. Getting into the suit requires an action (and, of course, access to your suit). Enabler.

Armor-Assisted Action. While wearing your special suit, you gain +1 to your Might Edge. Enabler.

All of your tier abilities related to your armor work only when you are wearing the armor. For example, the armor won't emit a blast of energy or fly unless you're inside the suit to control it.

Tier 2: Heads-Up Display (2+ Intellect points). Your armor comes with systems that help you make sense of, analyze, and use your weapons in your environment. For ten minutes, your vision range is increased to 5 miles (8 km). If you spend one level of Effort, you can also see through mundane materials (such as wood, concrete, plastic, and stone) to a short distance in false color images. If you spend two levels

of Effort, you can see through special materials (such as solid lead or other solid metal, advanced materials, "unobtainium," and so on) to an immediate distance in false color images; however, the GM might require you to succeed at an Intellect-based task first, depending on the material blocking your armor's sensors. Enabler.

Tier 3: Energy Blast (1+ Intellect point). You can emit a concussive blast of energy from your armor to attack a target within long range for 4 points of damage. Instead of applying Effort to decrease the difficulty or increase damage, you can apply Effort to increase the maximum number of targets, one per level applied. Alternatively, you can apply Effort to increase the range by a long distance for each level applied. Action.

Tier 4: Field-Reinforced Armor. You gain +1 to Armor (for a total of +3 to Armor) while in your special suit. Enabler.

Tier 5: Armored Flight (5+ Intellect points). You can modulate the concussive release of energy produced by your armor so well that you can fly for ten minutes. If you apply a level of Effort, you can carry another creature of your size or smaller with you. Action to activate.

Tier 6: Energy Cyclone (3+ Intellect points). You can emit a shower of concussive energy blasts from your armor that inflicts 2 points of damage each, allowing you to attack up to six different targets in close range in one round as a single action. Make a separate attack roll for each attack. You remain limited by the amount of Effort you can apply on one action, but because you make separate attacks, the targets' Armor applies to each of them. Anything that modifies your attack or damage applies to all attacks (positively or negatively). Action.

CHARACTER PORTRAITS

Character portraits on this and the following pages are designed to be printed out and used on your character sheet for inspiration and ideas. They fit as-is onto the official character sheets for The Strange but may be resized to fit other character sheets as needed.
© 2015 Monte Cook Games, LLC. Permission granted to copy or alter for personal use.

HERE
LIES

LESTER MOORE
FOUR SLUGS
FROM A 44
NO LES
NO MORE

INDEX